Quinoa
for families

Quinoa
for families

RENA PATTEN

NEW HOLLAND

To everyone who has discovered this wonderful grain, quinoa, and all its health benefits. This book is especially for you. I wish you good health and happiness always!

Contents

The Quinoa Family

I am thrilled to have the opportunity once again to show the many wonderful and beneficial ways to use quinoa—the supergrain—in the kitchen.

Since my last book on this wonderful grain, *Cooking with Quinoa*, I have been absolutely amazed at the interest shown to this tiny little grain. (I will refer to quinoa as a grain throughout this book as this is the term most commonly used but I must point out that quinoa is, in fact a seed. I will explain that more later on in the introduction.)

I have received so much positive feedback from so many people through my cooking demonstrations or promotional work and have been quite overwhelmed at just how many have become aware of and appreciate the huge health benefits of quinoa and have embraced the whole concept of adding it to their daily diet.

It has been great to hear repeatedly from people who have and use *Cooking with Quinoa* how it has helped them become aware of the many different ways that quinoa can be prepared in the everyday kitchen.

People tell me how much their health and that of their family has improved for the better since including quinoa in their diet.

Many have said that their medical practitioner, their dietitian or their naturopath suggested they include quinoa as part of their daily diet.

These comments have been made not only by people who have an intolerance to gluten and wheat, but from people of all walks of life who, for one reason or another, need to or just want to change their eating habits for their health.

They have been people who have been diagnosed with or who already have a certain illness where diet seems to play a very important role. Other people have been looking for a general alternative to eating rice and pasta and have actually lost weight by switching to quinoa. They also claim to be better able to manage and control their weight with the help of quinoa. And then, of course, there have been people that eat quinoa simply because they like it.

I was also very surprised at the number of people who have an intolerance to rice and have therefore welcomed the opportunity to not only have a substitute to use but a substitute that has numerous beneficial health qualities and that is actually good for you.

When I first decided to write a cookbook about quinoa, my main purpose was to bring awareness of the existence of this grain and particularly the health benefits associated with it and show the different ways that it can be used in your cooking. It is a very useful ingredient to use, particularly when cooking at the same time for a group of people with varied dietary needs.

The idea behind this book was two-fold: firstly, it was to create and share new quinoa recipes for all the family and secondly to take some old, very popular and much-loved family favourites and re-create them as much as possible using quinoa in either grain, flake or flour form. And as I have been told many times you can never have too many quinoa recipes.

For those of you who may be new to quinoa, you may be asking yoursel—what exactly is quinoa? Quinoa (pronounced Keen-Wah) is a tiny little grain, but not just any grain. It is a grain that is considered to be almost a complete food, being very high in protein, full of vitamins, totally gluten, wheat and cholesterol free, usually organic and of absolutely great benefit to everyone's diet. It is very easy to prepare and best of all it tastes delicious.

It is an ancient seed native to the Andes Mountains in South America. It has been around for over 5,000 years and is known to have been a staple food of the ancient civilisation of the Incas, having sustained them for centuries.

The Incas used quinoa to supplement their diet of potatoes and corn. It was commonly referred to as the 'mother grain' or 'gold of the Incas' and was considered sacred. It is still considered to be a very important food in South American kitchens. I refer to quinoa as the supergrain of the century.

As stated earlier, although most commonly referred to as a grain, quinoa is a seed. It is the seed of a leafy plant called *Chenopodium quinoa* of the Chenopodium/ Goosefoot plant family and is distantly related to the spinach plant. I like to refer to it as a grain because it straight away gives people a rough idea about the size of this grain, whereas a seed could suggest it is similar in size to the seed in a citrus fruit or an olive for instance.

Quinoa is a pure and complete grain and almost the perfect food as the degree of nutrition in each tiny grain is regarded as being quite potent.

It has the highest amount of protein of any grains and this unusually high amount of protein is actually a complete protein containing all nine essential amino acids, the only grain to contain all nine of the essential amino acids. The quality of this protein has been likened by the World Health Authority as being the closest to milk.

The amino acid composition is extremely well balanced and has a particularly high content of the amino acid lysine, which is essential in our diet for tissue repair and growth, making it a must for vegans and vegetarians who may be concerned about the level of protein in their daily diet.

It is also a very good source of manganese, magnesium, potassium, phosphorous, copper, zinc, vitamins E and B6, riboflavin, niacin and thiamine. It has more calcium than cow's milk, is an excellent antioxidant, is rich in dietary fibre and has more iron than any other grain. It also has the highest content of unsaturated fats and a lower ratio of carbohydrates than any other grain plus a low glycemic index level. The health benefits to be gained from this grain are truly enormous.

Quinoa has a huge range of uses and lends itself beautifully to so many dishes. When cooked it has a very delicate texture and is lovely in soups, sweets, makes wonderful salads, pasta, breads and delicious vegetarian and non-vegetarian meals. You can also make pastry for pies using quinoa flour. Just remember that pastry made with quinoa flour may go a little soggy after about two days. If there is any pie left over in my household after two days, I tend to re-heat the pie in the oven to crisp up the pastry and we have the pie warm.

I consider quinoa to be a perfect food for coeliac sufferers, vegans and vegetarians. Quinoa is very easy to prepare, easy to digest and most enjoyable to eat. It is very light on the stomach and you don't tend to feel heavy after eating a meal made with quinoa. I also find certain sweets prepared with quinoa flour can be lighter than those prepared with normal wheat flour.

To those who are gluten or wheat intolerant, quinoa is a food that can offer you a greater variety and selection of food for your table. There should be a packet of quinoa in every pantry.

What does quinoa look like?

The grain itself is tiny and round with a fine band around it ending in what looks like a minute 'tail'. As it cooks the 'tail' spirals out and almost detaches itself. It becomes very distinct from the rest of the grain in the shape of an outer white ring that is clearly visible. When cooked the grain becomes very soft in the centre while the 'tail' retains a bit of crunch giving it a texture all of its own.

When the grain is cooked it has a very delicate texture and it expands to almost four times its original volume.

There are many different varieties of quinoa and it is available in grain, flake and

flour form, making it suitable for cooking in many different ways. The colour of the grain can vary from white (opaque), pale yellow to red, purple, brown and black. The recipes in this book extensively use all forms of this wonderful grain in one way or another, showing you just how easy it is to use this supergrain.

It is available at most health food stores and in the health food section of the larger supermarkets. Some shops also stock quinoa milk.

Cooked quinoa is very distinctive in both taste and appearance and stands out from other grains. It has a lovely, slightly nutty, taste, which is unique. It can be used as an accompaniment to a meal (as you would use rice) or you can use it with other ingredients to make up a complete meal.

The distinctive nutty taste is more pronounced in the flour, giving it quite an earthy aroma. The flour can also be slightly bitter, which I find can be counterbalanced by the other sweeter or aromatic ingredients used in a recipe. The flakes are great—use them as a substitute for normal breadcrumbs, especially for stuffings and coatings.

How to prepare quinoa

Quinoa grows in arid climates, at high altitudes and in very poor soil. It is suggested that the survival of this plant over the centuries could be attributed to a soapy like substance called saponin, which creates a bitter coating on the grain and protects it from the harsh high altitude weather as well as any birds or insects.

This bitter soapy coating must be removed before cooking. Although most grain comes pre-washed and ready to cook, it is still a good idea to rinse it thoroughly before use to remove any residue of saponin.

Simply place the quinoa in a fine sieve and rinse under cold running water while rubbing it lightly between your fingertips. Drain well and it is ready to cook. Make sure that you do use a very fine sieve as the grains are so tiny they will otherwise go straight through a standard colander or strainer.

Quinoa cooks very quickly simmered in water, stock, juice or milk. One part quinoa, two parts liquid and 10 minutes in the saucepan are usually all that's needed to prepare quinoa as a basic cooked grain. However, you may need to cook the quinoa a little longer if the liquid used is denser than water, such as a sauce, stock or milk. The darker grains, the red and black varieties, can take a little longer to cook and tend to retain a little bit more of a crunch. Resting the cooked quinoa covered, for 5 to 10 minutes after cooking will ensure it is softer and fluffier. Use a fork to fluff up the quinoa after it has been cooked.

It can be cooked in the microwave although that's not my preferred method: I find it a bit too fiddly and it seems to take longer. To cook quinoa in the microwave, place one part quinoa to two parts liquid in a microwave-proof dish and cook on high for 7 minutes; stir, then cover with plastic wrap and stand for 7 to 8 minutes. Depending on your microwave you may need to vary the cooking time. You can also cook quinoa in a rice cooker the same as way as you would on the stove top—one part quinoa to two parts water cooked on the rice setting then rest, covered, for 5 to 10 minutes.

For an added nutty taste, you can toast the quinoa before cooking. Rinse and drain the quinoa well then dry-roast in a small, non-stick frying pan. When the grains start to pop, remove the pan from heat and transfer the quinoa to a saucepan with two parts liquid, bring to the boil, then reduce the heat and simmer, covered, for 10 minutes. You may be able to find ready-toasted quinoa in some shops.

You can also sprout quinoa by placing one part rinsed quinoa with three parts water in a jar with a lid and soak for about two hours; drain and rinse, then return to the jar with the lid on and leave to sprout. You must rinse them at least twice per day. They are very tiny sprouts and should be ready in about three days, but must be eaten immediately as they do not last. You can use the sprouts in salads.

To prepare the salads from this book you will need to cook the quinoa first and then combine with the other ingredients.

I make a lot of salads using quinoa so I tend to cook a large batch of the grain and leave it in the refrigerator to use as I need it. Quinoa cooked in water will keep in the refrigerator for up to a week. For most of the other recipes in this book where the grain is used, the grain is actually cooked with the other ingredients making them one-pot meals. Which coloured grain you wish to use in your cooking is totally up to you. I have specified a colour in only a few recipes and purely for visual appeal.

Cooking appliances

It is important to remember that all cooking appliances, especially ovens, vary in their cooking time so you may need to experiment with your own to work out the correct cooking time.

Also cooking time can vary depending on the grain used, temperature of your cooking appliance and believe it or not even the type and size of saucepan used.

For the one-pot meals I find the best utensil to use is a large, deep frying pan with a lid. It not only holds a large quantity of ingredients but it also distributes and cooks the quinoa with all the other ingredients more evenly over a larger cooking surface.

SOUPS

Curried Parsnip Soup

2 tbsp extra virgin olive oil

2 large onions, chopped

2 tbsp curry paste

1.5 kg (3 lb 5 oz) parsnips, peeled and
chopped

8 cups hot chicken or vegetable stock

salt and freshly ground black pepper

2/3 cup red quinoa, rinsed and drained

2 cups boiling water

juice of 1 lemon

cream, for serving

fresh chives, chopped, for garnish

Heat oil in a large heavy-based saucepan and sauté onion until soft.

Stir in the curry paste and cook for about 30 seconds.

Add the parsnips and stock and season with salt and pepper.

Bring to the boil, reduce the heat and simmer, covered, for about 30 minutes or until the parsnips are tender.

Purée the soup with a stick blender or food processor.

Return soup to the pot, stir in quinoa and water and bring back up to the boil. Reduce the heat, cover and simmer for about 30 minutes or until quinoa is cooked.

Stir in the lemon juice and serve with a dollop of cream and some chopped chives sprinkled on top.

Serves 8

Note: This is a lovely thick soup, especially if you love parsnips. There are not too many ingredients in this soup which allows the flavour of the parsnips to really come through with a subtle curry flavour.

Chorizo Sausage, Bean and Cabbage Soup

Heat oil in a large saucepan and sauté the chorizo sausage and onions until onion is soft and chorizo golden.

Stir in the garlic and paprika and cook for about 30 seconds.

Add the cabbage, stock and bay leaves and season with salt and pepper. Bring to the boil, reduce heat, cover and simmer for about 15 minutes.

Stir in the quinoa and continue simmering covered for another 15 minutes.

Add the beans and bring back to the boil. Reduce the heat, cover and simmer for 12–15 minutes until quinoa is cooked

Remove the bay leaf, stir in the chives, adjust the seasoning and serve.

1 tbsp extra virgin olive oil

3 chorizo sausages, diced

2 red onions, finely chopped

1–2 cloves garlic, finely chopped

2 tsp sweet paprika

4 cups Savoy cabbage, very finely shredded

8 cups hot chicken or vegetable stock

2 bay leaves

salt and pepper

3/4 cup quinoa, rinsed and drained

2 x 400 g (14 oz) cans of cannellini beans, rinsed and drained

3 tbsp fresh chives, chopped

Serves 6–8

Note: This is a thick and hearty soup perfect for those cold wintery nights. You can substitute the chorizo sausage with bacon or chicken. Or leave out the meat all together.

Creamy Mushroom Soup

2 tbsp olive oil
1 large onion, chopped
1 kg (2 lb 4 oz) mushrooms, sliced
2 cloves garlic, chopped
½ cup flat-leaf parsley, chopped
salt and freshly cracked pepper
6 cups hot chicken stock
½ cup quinoa, rinsed and drained
½ cup cream
parsley, chopped, for garnish

Heat oil in a large saucepan and sauté onion until soft and golden.

Add the mushrooms and garlic and cook until mushrooms have collapsed.

Stir in the parsley, season with salt and pepper and cook on medium heat for 1-2 minutes.

Pour in the chicken stock and bring to the boil. Reduce heat and simmer for 20 minutes.

Remove from the heat and purée soup with either a stick blender or a food processor. Meanwhile, rinse and drain quinoa.

Place soup back on the stove, bring to the boil and stir in quinoa, reduce heat and simmer, covered, for 15-20 minutes.

Serve garnished with a drizzle of cream and chopped parsley.

Serves 4-6

Note: Keep in mind that quinoa will continue to expand a little more after cooking. If you find that your soup is too thick for your liking just thin down with extra water or stock.

Thai Pumpkin Soup

Peel, de-seed and cube the pumpkin and set aside.

Remove and discard the tough outer layer of the lemongrass and finely chop the tender white part.

Place lemongrass, chillies, lime rind, garlic, ginger, coriander, turmeric, cumin and five spice powder, water and 1 tbsp oil into a food processor and process until a paste is formed.

Heat the remaining oil in a large saucepan and sauté onion until golden.

Stir in the paste and cook for 3–5 minutes until fragrant.

Add the pumpkin, stock, coconut milk and salt, bring to the boil then reduce heat and simmer, covered, for about 20 minutes.

Using a potato masher, mash the pumpkin while in the pot then stir in the quinoa and continue cooking for another 20–25 minutes until the quinoa is cooked. (You can purée soup if you prefer, but I like the texture you get in the soup by mashing).

Let the soup rest for 10 minutes or so before serving.

Serve garnished with a good squeeze of lime juice, slices of chilli and some coriander leaves.

Serves 6–8

1 kg (2 lb 4 oz) butternut pumpkin
2 sticks lemongrass
2 long red chillies, deseeded and sliced
rind of 2 limes
3–4 cloves garlic, roughly chopped
3 cm (1¼ in) piece of ginger, chopped
1 cup fresh coriander (cilantro) stalks
   and leaves, chopped
1 tsp ground turmeric
1½ tsp ground cumin
½ tsp Chinese five-spice powder or
   1 tsp garam masala
1 tbsp water
3 tbsp olive oil
1 large brown onion, finely chopped
6 cups hot chicken or vegetable stock
1 x 400 g (14 oz) coconut milk
salt, to taste
¾ cup quinoa, rinsed and drained

GARNISH
red chilli slices
fresh coriander (cilantro) leaves
lime juice

Mulligatawny Soup

Heat oil in a large saucepan and brown chicken on both sides. Remove from pan and set aside.

Add onion, potato, carrots and swedes to the pan and sauté until vegetables soften and start to take on some colour, about 5-8 minutes.

Stir in curry paste, cloves, nutmeg and season with salt and pepper then cook for 1-2 minutes.

Return chicken to the pan and pour in stock. Bring to the boil, reduce heat, cover and simmer for 30 minutes until chicken is cooked. Remove chicken from the pan, set aside and keep warm.

Add the quinoa to the soup, bring back to the boil, reduce heat, cover and simmer for 20-25 minutes until quinoa is cooked, stirring occasionally.

Remove and discard the bone from the chicken, then shred or chop meat and return to the soup,. Stir and heat through and serve with a good squeeze of lime juice. I like to serve this soup garnished with chopped, fresh red chillies.

2 tbsp olive oil
6 chicken thigh cutlets, skin removed
1 large onion, finely chopped
1 large potato, peeled and finely diced
2 large carrots, peeled and finely chopped
2 swedes, peeled and finely chopped
2 tbsp curry paste or powder
pinch of cloves
pinch of nutmeg
salt and freshly ground black pepper
8 cups chicken or vegetable stock
¾ cup quinoa, rinsed and drained
lime juice
red chillies, chopped, for garnish (optional)

22

Serves 6

Note: Chicken cutlets are the thigh with only the thick bone left in.

quinoa for families

Minestrone Soup

2 tbsp olive oil

1 large onion, chopped

3 carrots, diced

3 stalks celery, diced

2 potatoes, diced

1 x 400 g (14 oz) can diced tomatoes, undrained

8 cups hot vegetable stock

salt and freshly cracked pepper

3/4 cup red or black quinoa, rinsed and drained

3 zucchini (courgette), diced

2 small cabbage leaves, very finely shredded

1 x 400 g (14 oz) can borlotti beans, drained

1 cup frozen peas

3 tbsp parsley, finely chopped

parmesan, grated

Heat oil in a large heavy-based saucepan, add the onion, carrot and celery and sauté until soft, about 5 minutes.

Add the potatoes, tomatoes, stock and season with salt and pepper. Bring to the boil, reduce heat, cover and simmer for about 30 minutes.

Stir in the quinoa, zucchini and the cabbage and bring back to the boil. Reduce heat and simmer for another 30 minutes until quinoa is cooked. (The dark quinoa always takes longer to cook, especially when cooked in a liquid other than water).

Add the beans and peas bring back to the boil and simmer for another 5 minutes.

Stir in the parsley and serve with grated or shaved parmesan.

Serves 6–8

Note: This very hearty and well-known Italian soup, with its abundance of vegetables, is full of goodness especially more so with the inclusion of quinoa instead of traditional pasta. Add whatever vegetables you have available to you. Alternatively, you could make your own quinoa pasta using the recipe on page 172.

quinoa for families

Zucchini (Courgette), Tomato and Thyme Soup

2 tbsp olive oil

1 large leek, sliced, including the green tender parts

1 large onion, chopped

2 cloves garlic, chopped

1 x 400 g (14 oz) can peeled, diced tomatoes, undrained

1 kg (2 lb 4 oz) zucchini (courgette), diced

1 tbsp fresh thyme leaves

8 cups chicken or vegetable stock

salt and freshly cracked black pepper

2/3 cup quinoa, rinsed and drained

lemon juice, for serving

Heat oil in a large saucepan. Add the leek, onions and garlic and sauté until the vegetables collapse and are soft.

Stir in the tomatoes, zucchini and thyme. Pour in the stock and season with salt and pepper.

Bring to the boil, reduce the heat and simmer covered on low heat for about 25 minutes until the zucchini are tender.

Remove the soup from the heat and purée using a stick blender or food processor. Return the soup to the heat and bring back to the boil.

Add the quinoa, reduce the heat, cover, and simmer for about 15–20 minutes, stirring occasionally until the quinoa is cooked.

Serve with a good squeeze of lemon juice.

Serves 8

25

soups

Bacon, Pea and Leek Soup

2 tbsp extra virgin olive oil
250 g (9 oz) bacon, rind removed and
    cut into pieces
1 large leek, washed and trimmed
1 large onion, chopped
1 kg (2 lb 4 oz) frozen peas
8 cups hot chicken or vegetable stock
salt and freshly ground pepper
¾ cup quinoa, rinsed and drained

Heat oil in a large saucepan and cook bacon until browned and crispy but not dry or burnt. Remove from pan with a slotted spoon and set aside.

Chop the leek including the tender green part and add to the pan with the onion and sauté on low heat until lightly coloured and soft.

Increase heat to high and add the peas (straight from the freezer) and the stock. Season to taste and bring to the boil.

When boiling, reduce the heat to low, cover and simmer for about 15 minutes.

Purée the soup in a food processor or blender, return to the pot, increase heat to high and bring back to the boil.

Add the quinoa and the bacon, reduce heat and simmer for another 20 minutes until quinoa is cooked. Stir the pot occasionally.

I like to serve this soup with a drizzle of extra virgin olive oil and sometimes I might even cook up a little extra bacon for garnish.

Serves 6–8

Note: This soup is similar to the pea and ham soup that we all know and love except it's cooked in half the time and the addition of quinoa makes it hearty and filling. Wonderful for those cold, wintery days.

Sweet Potato Soup

Heat oil in a large saucepan and sauté onion until soft. Stir in the cumin, garlic, chilli and lemon zest and cook until fragrant.

Add the potato and stock and season to taste. Bring to the boil, reduce the heat, cover and simmer for 20–30 minutes until potato is tender.

Purée soup and bring back up to the boil, add the quinoa and extra water, reduce the heat, cover and simmer for 15–20 minutes until quinoa is cooked.

Stir in the garnish, check and adjust the seasoning. Serve with a good squeeze of lemon juice.

To make the garnish, heat the oil in a small frying pan and sauté the garlic until it just starts to change colour. Add the cumin and cook until it stars to bubble. Stir in the coriander and cook for a few seconds until the coriander starts to wilt, then pour the garnish into the soup.

1 tbsp olive oil

2 red onions, chopped

1 tbsp ground cumin

2 cloves garlic, chopped

1–2 long red chillies, de-seeded and chopped

zest of 1 lemon

1.5 kg (3 lb 5 oz) sweet potato, peeled and chopped into chunks

8 cups hot chicken or vegetable stock

salt and freshly cracked black pepper

¾ cup quinoa, rinsed and drained

2 cups boiling water, extra

GARNISH

2 tbsp extra virgin olive oil

1 large clove garlic, finely grated

2 tsp ground cumin

¾ cup fresh coriander (cilantro), finely chopped

lemon juice

Serves 6–8

SALADS

Preserved Lemon and Olive Salad

1 cup quinoa, rinsed and drained

2 cups vegetable or chicken stock

1 bay leaf

2 tbsp extra virgin olive oil

1 large onion, chopped

2 large carrots, chopped

2 cloves garlic, chopped

2 x 400 g (14 oz) cans red kidney beans
  or lentils, rinsed and drained

1 cup pitted Kalamata olives, halved

250 g (9 oz) cherry tomatoes, halved or
  left whole

2–3 tbsp preserved lemon, finely
  chopped

4 tbsp flat-leaf parsley, finely chopped

2 tbsp extra virgin olive oil

juice of 1–1½ lemons

salt and freshly cracked black pepper

Place quinoa in small saucepan with the stock and bay leaf, bring to the boil, then reduce the heat, cover and simmer for 10–12 minutes until all the stock is absorbed. Remove from heat and cool completely, remove and discard bay leaf.

Heat the oil in a large frying pan and sauté the onion and carrots until the onions soften but the carrots still retain some crunch.

Stir in the garlic and cook for about 30 seconds until fragrant, remove from the heat.

Mix together the quinoa, onion and carrot mix, beans or lentils, olives, tomatoes, preserved lemon and lots of parsley.

Add the oil and lemon juice and season to taste. Toss everything together and serve.

Serves 4–6

Note: When using preserved lemons, discard the soft centre and use only the rind (although, I sometimes use all of it). You can find them at all delicatessens and most supermarkets. They are great to have in your pantry and can be added to curries, casseroles, soups, used as a condiment and are especially tasty in Moroccan cooking.

32

Chickpea (Garbanzo Bean), Olive and Feta Salad

Place quinoa in a small saucepan with the water, bring to the boil, then reduce the heat, cover and simmer for about 10 minutes until all the water is absorbed. Remove from the heat and cool.

Combine the chickpeas with the olives, capsicums, onion and parsley, add the quinoa and mix well.

Whisk together the garlic, lemon juice, horseradish cream if used and olive oil, season with salt and pepper and then gently toss the dressing through the salad.

Scatter the feta on top and drizzle with extra virgin olive oil.

Serves 6

¾ cup quinoa, rinsed and drained
1½ cups water
2 x 400 g (14 oz) cans chickpeas (garbanzo beans), rinsed and drained
150 g (5 oz) stuffed green olives
280 g (10 oz) jar char-grilled capsicums (peppers), cut into strips
1 small red onion, finely chopped
½–1 cup flat-leaf parsley, roughly chopped
1 clove garlic, finely grated
juice of 1 lemon
1 tsp horseradish cream (optional)
¼ cup extra virgin olive oil
salt and freshly cracked black pepper
150 g (5 oz) feta cheese, crumbled
extra virgin olive oil, extra, to garnish

Chickpea (Garbanzo Bean), Cucumber and Olive Salad

1 cup quinoa, rinsed and drained

2 cups water

1 large red capsicum (bell pepper)

2 Lebanese cucumbers

2 x 400 g (14 oz) cans chickpeas (garbanzo beans), rinsed and drained

1 carrot, peeled and coarsely grated

½ cup pitted Kalamata olives

handful of flat-leaf parsley, finely chopped

salt and freshly cracked black pepper

3 tbsp extra virgin olive oil

1 tbsp white wine vinegar

Place quinoa in a small saucepan with the water, bring to the boil, reduce heat then cover and simmer for 10 minutes until the water is absorbed. Remove from heat and cool completely.

Remove the core from the capsicum and cut into cubes. Slice the cucumber into four lengthways and chop.

Place quinoa, capsicum and cucumber into a large bowl. Add the chickpeas, carrot, olives, parsley, salt and pepper, olive oil and vinegar.

Toss well and serve. If possible, refrigerate for about 30 minutes before serving.

Serves 4–6

36

Roast Pumpkin and Lentil Salad

Pre-heat oven to 190°C (375°F) and line a baking tray with non-stick baking paper.

Peel and chop pumpkin into small pieces, season with a little salt and drizzle with extra virgin olive oil. Bake until cooked and charred along the edges (about 20 minutes). Remove from oven and cool.

Meanwhile place the quinoa in a small saucepan with the water, bring to the boil, then reduce the heat, cover and simmer for 10 minutes until all the water is absorbed. Remove from the heat and cool completely.

Place pumpkin and lentils into a mixing bowl; gently stir in the quinoa, onion, spring onions and coriander.

Dry-roast the cumin seeds in a small frying pan until they become fragrant and start to pop. Remove from heat and grind to a fine powder in a mortar and pestle.

To make the dressing, mix the cumin together with all the other dressing ingredients, pour over salad and gently toss through.

Serves 4–6

1.5 kg (3 lb 5 oz) butternut pumpkin
salt
1–2 tbsp extra virgin olive oil
¾ cup quinoa, rinsed and drained
1½ cups water
2 x 400 g (14 oz) cans brown lentils, rinsed and drained
1 medium red onion, finely sliced
4 spring onions (scallions), chopped
½ cup fresh coriander (cilantro), chopped

DRESSING
1 tsp cumin seeds
zest and juice of 1 lemon
3–4 tbsp extra virgin olive oil
salt and pepper, to taste

Orange, Ginger, Carrot and Coconut Salad

¾ cup black quinoa, rinsed and drained

1¾ cups water

4 medium carrots, peeled and coarsely grated

½ cup golden sultanas or raisins

¾ cup shredded coconut

3 tbsp chives, chopped

juice of 1 orange, strained

grated rind of 1 orange

1 tbsp ginger, freshly grated

2 tbsp extra virgin olive oil

2–3 tbsp lime juice

salt and freshly ground black pepper

Place quinoa in a small saucepan with the water, bring to the boil, then reduce the heat, cover and simmer for 12–15 minutes until all the water is absorbed and quinoa tender. Remove from the heat and cool completely.

Place the carrots, raisins, coconut and chives into a large bowl and stir in the cooled quinoa.

Whisk together the orange juice and rind with the ginger, oil, lime juice, salt and pepper. Toss well and, if possible, place in the refrigerator for about 1 hour before serving.

Serves 4–6

Tomato and Mozzarella Pesto Salad

Place quinoa in a small saucepan with the water, bring to the boil, then reduce the heat, cover and simmer for 10 minutes until all the water is absorbed. Remove from the heat and cool completely.

To make the pesto, place basil, garlic, pine nuts and cheese into a food processor or blender. With the motor on pulse mode, slowly pulse the ingredients and pour in enough oil until you get a creamy and soft consistency that still has a little texture to it.

Season to taste and add more cheese or oil if needed according to your preference. If feeling particularly energetic you can use a mortar and pestle to make the sauce.

Place the quinoa into a bowl and mix in the pesto sauce really well so as to completely coat the quinoa.

Leave the tomatoes whole or cut in half and roughly tear the cheese open without cutting through completely. Toss the tomatoes and mozzarella through the quinoa.

Squeeze some lemon juice on top and serve garnished with shavings of parmesan, basil leaves and a light drizzle of extra virgin olive oil.

1½ cups quinoa, rinsed and drained
3 cups water
250 g (9 oz) grape or cherry tomatoes
220 g (8 oz) baby bocconcini cheese
lemon juice
olive oil, extra
parmesan, shaved
basil leaves, for garnish

PESTO SAUCE
1 large bunch basil leaves
2 cloves garlic, chopped
90 g (3 oz) pine nuts
½–¾ cup parmesan, freshly grated
½ cup extra virgin olive oil (approx.)
salt and pepper

Serves 4–6

41

salads

Black Bean, Capsicum (Bell Pepper) and Chilli Salad

¾ cup quinoa, rinsed and drained

1½ cups water

1 x 440 g (15 oz) can black beans, rinsed and drained

1 large red capsicum (bell pepper), seeded and cut into pieces

4 spring onions (scallions), sliced diagonally

1–2 red chillies, seeded and chopped or sliced

3 tbsp flat-leaf parsley, chopped

zest and juice of 1 large lemon

3–4 tbsp extra virgin olive oil

salt and freshly cracked black pepper

Place quinoa in a small saucepan with the water, bring to the boil, then reduce the heat, cover and simmer for about 10 minutes until all the water is absorbed. Remove from the heat and cool completely.

When cold, place quinoa in a bowl with the beans, capsicum, spring onions, chillies and parsley.

Add the lemon zest and juice, olive oil and season to taste.

Salad is best if prepared in advance and all the flavours have a chance to develop.

Serves 4–6

Borlotti Bean, Tomato and Basil Salad

½ cup black quinoa

½ cup white quinoa

2 cups water

2 x 400 g (14 oz) cans borlotti beans, rinsed and drained

2 celery stalks, diced

250 g (9 oz) grape or cherry tomatoes, left whole or halved

1 red onion, finely chopped

2 cloves garlic, finely grated

2 tbsp capers

8–12 basil leaves, torn into small pieces

2 tbsp chives, chopped

salt and freshly cracked pepper

2 tbsp lemon juice

4 tbsp extra virgin olive oil

1½ tbsp red wine vinegar

Place both types of quinoa into a small saucepan with the water, bring to the boil, then reduce the heat, cover and simmer for 12–15 minutes until all the water is absorbed. Remove from heat and cool completely. (You may need to cook the quinoa for a little longer as the dark variety can take longer to cook.)

Place cooled quinoa into a large bowl and add the beans, celery including some of the young tender leaves, tomatoes, onion, garlic, capers, basil and chives.

Season with salt and pepper to taste then add the lemon juice, oil and vinegar. Toss well and serve.

You can use this salad as a main meal or as a side dish with meat, chicken or fish. Great for a barbeque.

Serves 4–6

Cucumber and Dill Salad

Place both types of quinoa in a small saucepan with the water, bring to the boil then reduce heat, cover and simmer for about 10-13 minutes until all the water is absorbed and the quinoa is cooked. Cooking time will vary as the red quinoa takes a little longer to cook than the white. Remove from the heat and cool completely.

Place cooled quinoa into a bowl with the cucumbers, pickled cucumbers, onion, dill and chives. Season with salt and pepper then add the oil and vinegar and toss well.

If possible, leave for about 20-30 minutes before serving. Great as a side salad with grilled or pan-fried fish, or any meat.

Serves 4

½ cup white quinoa
½ cup red quinoa
2 cups water
3 medium-large Lebanese cucumbers, cut in four lengthways and chopped
2 pickled dill cucumbers, chopped into small pieces
1 medium red onion, finely chopped
3 tbsp fresh dill, finely chopped
3 tbsp chives, finely chopped
salt and freshly ground black pepper
¼ cup extra virgin olive oil
1 tbsp red wine vinegar

Artichoke and Rocket (Arugula) Salad

Place quinoa in a small saucepan with the water, bring to the boil, then reduce the heat, cover and simmer for 10 minutes until all the water is absorbed. Remove from heat and cool.

Place quinoa in a bowl with the artichokes, beans, olives, shallots and rocket leaves and gently toss together to combine.

Whisk together the horseradish cream, garlic, red wine vinegar and olive oil. Season with salt and pepper.

Pour dressing over the salad and gently toss to combine.

Serves 4–8

1 cup quinoa, rinsed and drained
2 cups water
2 x 280 g (10 oz) jars artichoke hearts, drained and halved
2 x 400 g (14 oz) cans borlotti beans, rinsed and drained
1 cup pitted Kalamata olives, halved
6 spring onions (scallions), sliced
200 g (7 oz) rocket (arugula) leaves

DRESSING
1 tbsp horseradish cream
1 clove garlic, finely grated
1–2 tbsp red wine vinegar
3–4 tbsp extra virgin olive oil
salt and freshly ground black pepper

Roasted Sweet Potato, Spinach and Mushroom Salad

1 kg (2 lb 4 oz) sweet potato
1–2 tbsp extra virgin olive oil
salt and pepper
¾ cup red quinoa, rinsed and drained
1½ cups water
200 g (7 oz) baby spinach leaves
250 g (9 oz) mushrooms, sliced
1 red onion, halved and thinly sliced

DRESSING
2 tbsp Dijon mustard
juice of 1–2 lemons
½ cup extra virgin olive oil
salt and freshly ground black pepper

Preheat oven to 180°C (350°F) and line a baking tray with non-stick baking paper.

Peel and cube sweet potato, drizzle with olive oil and season with salt and pepper. Toss well and place on the baking tray in a single layer.

Roast in the oven for 20–30 minutes until potato is tender and browned.

In the meantime, place quinoa in a small saucepan with the water, bring to the boil, then reduce the heat, cover and simmer for 10–12 minutes until all the water is absorbed. Remove from heat and cool.

Place sweet potato, quinoa, spinach, mushroom and onion in a bowl and gently toss together until combined.

Mix together all dressing ingredients, pour over salad and gently toss. Leave to stand for about ½ hour before serving.

Serves 4–8

Note: This is a big and hearty salad and is a meal on its own. The number of serves depends on whether you are serving it on its own or as a side dish.

Mango Salad

Place quinoa in a small saucepan with the water and lime rind, bring to the boil, then reduce the heat, cover and simmer for 10 minutes until all the water is absorbed. Remove from heat and cool completely, remove and discard rind.

Combine the quinoa in a bowl with the cucumbers, spring onions, chillies and coriander leaves. Finely chop some of the coriander stems and use them as well.

Mix, or better still pound, all of the dressing ingredients together in a mortar and pestle. Pour dressing over the salad, toss well and just before serving, add the mango and garnish with extra coriander leaves.

If you plan to prepare this salad in advance it is best that you add the mango to the salad just before serving. It can go quite soggy if it is added too far in advance.

Serves 4

Note: You can make this salad as a main meal by adding cooked chicken or prawns—really delicious!

¾ cup quinoa
1½ cups water
1 large piece of lime rind
2 Lebanese cucumbers, diced
4 spring onions (scallions), sliced
2 long red chillies, deseeded and sliced
½ cup coriander (cilantro) leaves, chopped
1–2 large mangoes, peeled and diced
coriander (cilantro) leaves, for garnish

DRESSING
zest of 1 lime
1 clove garlic, finely grated
1 tsp palm or brown sugar
1 tbsp fish sauce
juice of 1–2 limes
1 tbsp extra virgin olive oil

51

Tuna Salad

1 cup quinoa, rinsed and drained

2 cups water

1 red capsicum (bell pepper), cut into chunks

1 green capsicum (bell pepper), cut into chunks

2 Lebanese cucumbers, diced

6 spring onions (scallions), sliced

3 tbsp parsley, finely chopped

2–3 tbsp capers, drained

15–20 pitted Kalamata olives, halved

2 x 400 g (14 oz) cans cannellini beans, rinsed and drained

1 x 400 g (14 oz) can tuna chunks in spring water or oil, drained

1½ tbsp red wine vinegar

3 tbsp extra virgin olive oil

salt and freshly ground black pepper

Place quinoa in a small saucepan with the water, bring to the boil, then reduce the heat, cover and simmer for 10 minutes until all the water is absorbed. Remove from heat and cool completely.

Combine the quinoa with the capsicum, cucumbers, spring onions, parsley, capers, olives and beans in a bowl and toss well.

Drain the tuna and add to the salad: you can use either tuna in spring water or oil, totally up to you.

Whisk together the vinegar, oil, salt and pepper. Pour over salad and toss through.

Serves 4–6

Note: This is my son's favourite salad and he takes it to work two to three times every week. It is filling and satisfying. I often have it in the fridge and everyone uses it as a meal on the run or just as a quick snack.

Asparagus, Pea and Mint Salad with Parmesan

Place quinoa in a small saucepan with the water, bring to the boil, then reduce the heat, cover and simmer for 12–15 minutes until all the water is absorbed. Remove from the heat and cool completely.

Trim the asparagus by removing and discarding some of the bottom part of the stem then cut asparagus into smallish pieces and blanch in boiling, lightly salted water for 2 minutes only.

Drain and place in iced water to stop cooking process.

Drain peas and place in a bowl with the quinoa, asparagus, mint and onion.

Whisk together the olive oil, mustard, vinegar, salt and pepper and pour over salad.

Add the parmesan and toss well. Serve with extra parmesan shavings.

¾ cup red quinoa

1½ cups water

2 bunches young, pencil-thin asparagus

500 g (17½ oz) cooked peas

3 tbsp fresh mint, chopped

1 medium red onion, chopped

4 tbsp extra virgin olive oil

1 tbsp Dijon mustard

2 tbsp red wine vinegar

salt and freshly cracked pepper

½ cup parmesan, grated

Serves 6

Note: Don't be tempted to cut off too much of the stems from the asparagus as this can be wasteful, especially if you use the very young and thin ones.

Coleslaw

Place quinoa in a small saucepan with the water, bring to the boil, then reduce the heat, cover and simmer for 10-14 minutes until all the water is absorbed and the quinoa is tender. Remove from heat and cool completely.

Combine the quinoa, cabbages, carrots, onion and celery in a large bowl and mix really well—your hands are probably the best mixing tool for this salad.

Stir through the mayonnaise, vinegar and olive oil, season with salt and pepper and toss until well coated.

Cover and chill for several hours before serving.

Serves 8-10

Note: This makes a large salad and is great for a crowd. The quinoa adds an extra crunch and texture, especially as I have used the black quinoa, which tends to remain crunchier than the white one.

1 cup black quinoa, rinsed and drained
2 cups water
¼ small white cabbage, trimmed and finely shredded
¼ small red cabbage, trimmed and finely shredded
2 carrots, coarsely grated
1 red onion, halved and finely sliced
2 stalks celery, finely sliced
salt and freshly cracked pepper
⅓ cup mayonnaise
2 tbsp red wine vinegar
2 tbsp extra virgin olive oil

VEGETARIAN

Three-Veg Bake

½ cup quinoa, rinsed and drained
1 cup water
500 g (17½ oz) broccoli, cooked
500 g (17½ oz) pumpkin, cooked
500 g (17½ oz) yellow squash, cooked
90 g (3 oz) butter
6 tbsp quinoa flour
3 cups milk
1 cup tasty or mild cheddar cheese, grated
2 tbsp parmesan, grated
salt and freshly cracked pepper
ground paprika

Place quinoa into a small saucepan with the water, bring to the boil, then reduce the heat, cover and simmer for 10 minutes or until all the water is absorbed. Remove from the heat and cool slightly.

Preheat oven to 200°C (400°F).

Place quinoa, broccoli, pumpkin and squash (or combination of other favourite vegetables) into a large bowl.

Melt butter in a medium-sized saucepan, add the flour and stir to form a roux. Cook for about 1 minute so as to cook out the raw taste of the flour.

Slowly pour in the milk and continue stirring until the mixture thickens and starts to bubble.

Stir in the cheese and cook for another minute or so until the cheese melts.

Pour the sauce over the vegetables and quinoa and gently toss to mix together. Taste and adjust seasoning.

Place in a baking dish, sprinkle with a little extra pepper and paprika and bake for 30 minutes until really golden and bubbly.

Serves 4–6

Note: This is a great dish to serve with the Steak with Mushroom Gravy (page 101). A different take on the much-loved steak and three-veg dish.

59

vegetarian

Mushroom and Cheese Pie

2 tbsp olive oil

4 spring onions (scallions), sliced
   (including the green parts)

450 g (15 oz) mushrooms, sliced

2 cloves garlic, finely chopped

2 tbsp flat-leaf parsley, chopped

6 large eggs

300 ml (10¼ fl oz) cream

300 ml (10¼ fl oz) full-cream milk

⅔ cup quinoa flour

1 tsp gluten-free baking powder

1 cup grated tasty or mild cheddar
   cheese

salt and freshly cracked pepper

Preheat oven to 180°C (350°F) and lightly grease an ovenproof baking dish.

Heat oil in a frying pan and sauté spring onions for 1–2 minutes until they soften.

Add the mushrooms and continue cooking on high heat until the mushrooms have collapsed and have taken on a golden colour.

Stir in the garlic and parsley, cook for another minute then remove from heat.

Whisk the eggs in a bowl with the cream and milk until well combined. Sift the flour and the baking powder together then stir into the egg mixture with the cheese and season with salt and pepper.

Place the mushroom mix into the prepared baking dish then pour over the egg mixture.

Bake for 40–45 minutes until the pie is set and golden.

Rest for at least 10 minutes before cutting and serving with a salad.

Serves 4

Creamed Spinach

500 g (17½ oz) frozen spinach, thawed
60 g (2 oz) butter
4 tbsp quinoa flour
2 cups milk
¾ cup tasty or mild cheddar cheese,
   grated
2 tbsp parmesan, grated
salt and freshly ground black pepper

Cook thawed spinach covered in the microwave for about 5 minutes or until cooked, then place in a fine sieve. Using the back of a spoon press to drain off all the excess moisture from the spinach then set aside.

Melt butter in a small saucepan, add the flour and stir to form a roux. Keep stirring for about 1 minute as you want to cook off the raw taste of the flour.

Slowly pour in the milk and continue to stir until the mixture thickens and starts to bubble.

Stir in the tasty and parmesan and cook for another minute or so until the cheese melts.

Stir in the spinach and cook on low heat for 2–3 minutes.

Season with salt and pepper to taste.

Serves 4

Note: This is a great side dish and a really good way to get the kids to eat their spinach. My children used to love this when they were little. If using fresh spinach, cook it first and use more to get the amount required as it will wilt down once cooked.

62

Chilli Beans

Heat oil in a large frying pan and sauté onion until soft and golden. Add the garlic and cook for about 30 seconds until fragrant. Stir in the paprika, oregano, cumin and chilli flakes.

Add the tomatoes, cover and simmer on low heat for about 5 minutes.

Stir in the quinoa, water and salt. Bring to the boil, reduce the heat, cover and simmer for 15 minutes.

Add the beans and cook for another 5–10 minutes until the beans have heated through and the quinoa is cooked.

Stir in the fresh coriander and it is ready to serve with a squeeze of lime juice and a dollop of sour cream or yoghurt.

Serves 4

Note: To make this dish vegan, use a non-dairy yoghurt or sour cream.

2 tbsp extra virgin olive oil
1 large red onion, chopped
3 cloves garlic
2 tsp ground sweet paprika
2 tsp ground oregano
1½ tbsp ground cumin
½–1 tsp dried chilli flakes
1 x 400 g (14 oz) can diced tomatoes
1½ cups quinoa, rinsed and drained
2½ cups boiling water
pinch of salt
2 x 400 g (14 oz) cans red kidney beans, rinsed
½ cup coriander (cilantro) leaves, chopped
lime juice
sour cream or Greek yoghurt, for serving

Lemon, Ginger, Turmeric and Curry Leaf Pilaf

Place quinoa into a medium-sized saucepan with the water, bring to the boil, then reduce the heat, cover and simmer for 10 minutes until all the water is absorbed. Remove from heat.

Heat oil in a large frying pan, add the mustard seeds and cook on medium-high heat until they start to pop,

Add the ginger, garlic and chilli flakes and cook until fragrant, about 1-2 minutes, then stir in the turmeric and season with salt.

Lightly crush the curry leaves to release their natural oil and add to the pan, cook 1-2 minutes until they start to release their fragrance and collapse.

Stir in the quinoa and lemon juice and mix really well until everything is thoroughly combined and heated through.

Garnish with the fresh chillies if used and serve the pilaf on its own or as a side dish.

Serves 4-6

2 cups quinoa, rinsed and drained
4 cups water
2 tbsp olive oil
1 tbsp black mustard seeds
1-2 tbsp ginger, grated
3 cloves garlic, grated
½-1 tsp dried chilli flakes
1 tsp ground turmeric
salt
handful of fresh curry leaves
juice of 1-2 lemons
fresh red chillies, sliced, for garnish
   (optional)

65

vegetarian

Spiced Lentils with Spinach

1 cup quinoa, rinsed and drained

2 cups water

3 tbsp olive oil

1 large onion, chopped

3 cloves garlic, chopped

1½ tbsp ground cumin

1 tbsp ground coriander (cilantro)

½–1 tsp chilli flakes or to taste

1 x 400 g (14 oz) can diced tomatoes,
  undrained

2 x 400 g (14 oz) cans lentils, undrained

salt, to taste

200 g (7 oz) baby spinach

natural or Greek yoghurt, for serving

lemon juice, for serving

Place quinoa in a small saucepan with the water and bring to the boil. Reduce the heat, cover and simmer for 10 minutes until all the water is absorbed.

Heat oil in a large, deep frying pan and sauté onion until it is lightly browned.

Stir in the garlic and cook for about 30 seconds until fragrant, take the pan off the heat and stir in the cumin, coriander and chilli, add a little more oil to the pan if it's too dry.

Return the pan to the heat and cook spices for about 30 seconds, stirring constantly so that the spices don't burn.

Add the tomatoes and lentils and season with salt. Bring to the boil, reduce the heat, cover and simmer for about 10 minutes.

Throw in the spinach and cook until it wilts, then stir in the quinoa, heat through and serve with a dollop of Greek yoghurt and a squeeze of lemon juice.

Serves 4

Note: It's a good idea to always have some cooked quinoa in the refrigerator, ready to use. This is one of those quick nourishing meals you can just throw together when you get home from work, especially if you have pre-cooked quinoa. You can use frozen spinach, just add it at the same stage as lentils.

Chickpea (Garbanzo Bean) and Vegetable Curry

Heat oil in a large saucepan and sauté onions until they are soft and golden. Add the garlic and chilli and cook until fragrant.

Stir in the curry paste, cumin and cardamom pods and cook for about one minute.

Wash the coriander really well and finely chop the roots and stalks and add to the pot, reserving the leaves for later. Add the cauliflower, pumpkin and chickpeas.

Pour in the coconut milk and water, season with salt and pepper then stir in the quinoa.

Bring to the boil, reduce the heat, cover and simmer for about 30 minutes until all the vegetables are tender and quinoa is cooked. Give the curry a gentle stir every now and then.

Stir in the peas and simmer for another 5 minutes.

Roughly chop the coriander leaves and add to the curry with a good squeeze of lemon or lime juice then let the curry stand for a good 10 minutes before serving with a dollop of Greek yoghurt.

Serves 6–8

Note: Serve without the yoghurt to make this recipe vegan-friendly.

2 tbsp extra virgin olive oil

2 large onions, peeled, halved then sliced

4 cloves garlic, chopped

1 long red chilli, de-seeded and chopped

2 tbsp mild curry paste

1 tsp ground cumin

6 cardamom pods, crushed

½ bunch fresh coriander (cilantro), roots, stalks and leaves

½ head cauliflower, approx. 750 g (26½ oz), cut into florets

½ butternut pumpkin, approx. 750 g (26½ oz), cut into chunks

2 x 400 g (14 oz) cans chickpeas (garbanzo beans), rinsed and drained

1 x 400 g (14 oz) can coconut milk

3 cups hot water

salt and freshly cracked pepper

1⅓ cups quinoa, rinsed and drained

1 cup frozen peas

lemon or lime juice

Greek yoghurt, for serving

vegetarian

Wild Mushrooms with Wine and Garlic

2 tbsp extra virgin olive oil

1 kg (2 lb 4 oz) selection of wild
mushrooms

1 large brown onion, finely chopped

4 spring onions (scallions), sliced

3 cloves garlic, finely chopped

½ cup white wine

1½ cups quinoa grain, rinsed and
drained

2½ cups hot water

salt and freshly cracked black pepper

½ cup flat-leaf parsley, finely chopped

parmesan, shaved

Heat oil in a large, deep-sided frying pan. Slice the larger mushrooms and leave any tiny ones whole then toss in the oil and cook until they have collapsed and are soft, about 3–5 minutes.

Remove the mushrooms from the pan with a slotted spoon and set aside.

Add onion and spring onions to the pan and sauté until golden; add a little more oil to the pan if necessary.

Stir in the garlic and cook for a few seconds then pour in the wine and deglaze the pan. Cook for about 1–2 minutes until the alcohol evaporates.

Add the quinoa, one-third of the mushrooms and the water.

Season with salt and pepper then bring to the boil, reduce the heat, cover and simmer for about 12–15 minutes until all the water is absorbed and the quinoa is cooked.

Toss in the parsley and remaining mushrooms and serve with shavings of parmesan.

Serves 4

Note: You can use a combination of a variety of mushrooms or you can use just one type—it really doesn't matter. I usually choose a combination of ordinary field mushrooms, Swiss brown, fresh shiitake, Portobello, oyster or enoki. Any type of mushroom works really well.

quinoa for families

Cauliflower Patties

Cook cauliflower in boiling salted water until quite tender. Drain well and place into a bowl to cool.

Chop the cauliflower into small pieces and then, using a fork, lightly mash. Mix in the spring onions, eggs, parsley, garlic, cumin, salt and pepper. Stir in the flour and mix to combine.

Heat oil in a frying pan until medium-hot, drop spoonfuls of cauliflower into the oil and cook until golden on both sides. Remove from pan with a slotted spoon and drain on kitchen paper towels.

These are best eaten hot or warm.

500 g (17½ oz) cauliflower florets
3 spring onions (scallions), sliced
2 eggs, lightly beaten
2 tbs flat-leaf parsley, finely chopped
1–2 cloves garlic, finely grated
1 heaped tsp ground cumin
salt and freshly ground black pepper
½ cup quinoa flour
olive oil, for shallow frying

Makes about 15–18

Note: Apart from being a family favourite, I have to say these patties are one of my absolute favourite vegetable dishes. I make them on a regular basis, especially in winter when the cauliflowers are at their best. I find this is also a great way to get kids to eat cauliflower as they love them. These patties are lovely served with a chutney or a sweet chilli dipping sauce.

Pine Nut and Sultana Pilaf

150 g (5 oz) pine nuts
1 tbsp extra virgin olive oil
1 tbsp ghee (clarified butter)
1 large brown onion, finely chopped
2 cloves garlic, finely chopped
2 cups quinoa, rinsed and drained
¾ cup sultanas or golden raisins
4 cups hot chicken or vegetable stock
salt and freshly ground black pepper
3 tbsp flat-leaf parsley, finely chopped
lemon juice, for serving

Dry-roast pine nuts in a small non-stick frying pan until lightly browned. Remove from the pan and set aside. Don't be tempted to leave them in the pan as they will continue to brown in the residual heat.

Heat oil and ghee in a large, deep frying pan and sauté onions until soft and just start to change colour. Add the garlic and cook for 30 seconds until fragrant.

Stir in the quinoa and sultanas, making sure you coat them well in the oil and onion mixture. Pour in the hot stock and season with a little salt and pepper; keep in mind the saltiness of the stock.

Bring to the boil, reduce heat, cover, and simmer for about 15–17 minutes or until all the liquid is absorbed.

Using a fork, stir in the pine nuts and parsley, cover and leave for 3–5 minutes before serving with a squeeze of lemon juice.

Serves 4

Eggplant (Aubergine) with Mint and Pine Nuts

1 kg (2 lb 4 oz) eggplant (aubergine),
  cut into large cubes
extra virgin olive oil
1 cup quinoa, rinsed and drained
2 cups water
2 tbsp extra virgin olive oil, extra
90 g (3 oz) pine nuts
1 large red onion, chopped
2 cloves garlic, chopped
½ cup fresh mint, chopped
2 tbsp red wine vinegar
salt and freshly cracked black pepper

Preheat oven to 180°C (350°F) and line a baking tray with non-stick baking paper.

Coat the eggplant with some oil and season with salt and pepper. Place on the baking tray and bake for about 20 minutes or until browned.

Meanwhile place quinoa in a small saucepan with the water, bring to the boil, then reduce the heat, cover and simmer for 10 minutes or until all the water is absorbed.

Heat the extra oil in a large frying pan and sauté the onion until soft, add the garlic and cook for 30 seconds until fragrant. Stir in the mint and the vinegar.

Add the quinoa, eggplant and pine nuts to the pan, season with salt and pepper and toss well to combine.

Serves 4–6

Note: For added crunch, you can toast the pine nuts in a non-stick frying pan. I prefer not to in this dish as they tend to taste creamier if they are not toasted.

quinoa for families

Pesto Quinoa

Place quinoa in a small saucepan with the water, bring to the boil, then reduce the heat, cover and simmer for 10 minutes until all the water is absorbed. Remove from the heat.

Make the pesto by placing the basil, including some of the tender stalks, garlic, pine nuts and cheese into a food processor or blender.

With the motor on pulse mode, slowly pulse the ingredients and pour in the lemon juice and enough oil until you get a creamy and soft consistency with a little texture in it.

Season to taste and add more cheese or oil if needed according to your taste. If feeling particularly energetic you can use a mortar and pestle to make the pesto sauce.

Place the quinoa into a bowl while still hot. Add the pesto sauce and, using two forks, gently toss together so as to completely coat the quinoa.

Serve with shavings of parmesan and a light drizzle of extra virgin olive oil.

1½ cups quinoa, rinsed and drained
3 cups water
parmesan shavings, for garnish
basil leaves, for garnish
olive oil, for garnish

PESTO
1 large bunch basil leaves
2 cloves garlic, chopped
90 g (3 oz) pine nuts
½–¾ cup parmesan, freshly grated
2 tsp lemon juice
½ cup extra virgin olive oil (approx.)
salt and pepper

Serves 4

Note: This is one of my favourite ways to serve quinoa and you can serve this warm or cold. Alternatively, you can turn it into a salad by tossing some grape or cherry tomatoes and chunks of mozzarella cheese through the quinoa (see page 41).

75

Zucchini (Courgette) Slice

Preheat oven to 180°C (350°F) and lightly grease a medium-sized 20 x 30 cm (8 x 12 in) baking dish.

Combine the zucchini with the onion, spring onions, eggs and oil.

Mix in the cheese and chillies if used and season with salt and pepper to taste.

Sift the flour with the baking powder and bicarb soda then fold into the zucchini mixture. Mix until thoroughly combined.

Pour into the baking dish and bake for about 40–45 minutes until golden brown and set.

Serves 6

Note: I make this dish on a regular basis, but I don't always make it as a whole slice. I very often make it as muffins and whenever we have a gathering where finger food is served I always make this as little mini muffins. They are always, always a huge success. These are ideal for parties as they cater for everyone, including vegetarians and anyone who may have an intolerance to gluten (as long as they are made with gluten-free baking powder) and/or wheat.

3 large zucchini (courgette), coarsely grated

1 onion, grated

4 spring onions (scallions), finely sliced

6 eggs

⅓ cup olive oil

1 cup tasty or mild cheddar cheese, grated

1–2 long red chillies, de-seeded and finely chopped (optional)

1 cup quinoa flour

1 tsp gluten-free baking powder

1 tsp bicarbonate soda (baking soda)

salt and freshly cracked pepper

vegetarian

POULTRY

Parmesan and Herb-crusted Chicken Schnitzel

4 halves chicken breast fillets

1½ cups quinoa flakes

¾ cup parmesan, grated

2 tbsp basil, finely chopped

2 tbsp chives, finely chopped

2 tbsp parsley, finely chopped

grated rind of 1 lemon

salt and freshly cracked black pepper

⅓–½ cup quinoa flour

2 eggs, lightly beaten

olive oil, for frying

lemon juice, for serving

Place the chicken breast half between two sheets of plastic wrap and gently pound with a meat mallet or rolling pin until about 5 mm (¼ in) thick. If the pieces of chicken are too big then cut each one in half.

Combine quinoa flakes with the cheese, herbs, lemon rind, salt and pepper.

Dust each piece of chicken with flour then dip into the beaten egg. Gently press into the flake mixture to coat well.

Heat some olive oil in a large frying pan and shallow-fry the chicken pieces in batches until golden and cooked. Drain on kitchen paper.

Serve with a good squeeze of lemon juice and a lovely salad.

Serves 4

Chicken and Leeks in a Creamy Mustard Sauce with Herbed Quinoa

Prepare leeks by washing and removing all dirt and grit that is normally lodged between all the layers then slice thinly, including some of the more tender green parts.

Heat oil in a large, deep frying pan until hot, add the chicken and brown on both sides. Remove from pan, cover and keep warm. Add leeks to the pan and sauté until tender, stir in garlic and cook for about 30 seconds until fragrant.

Stir in mustard, then add wine and the thyme. Return chicken to pan and cook for about 1–2 minutes until the alcohol evaporates.

Season then add the cream, stir well and bring to the boil. Reduce heat, cover and simmer for about 15 minutes until chicken is completely cooked and sauce has thickened. If sauce is too runny, cook, uncovered, for another 2 minutes or so until the sauce has thickened. Serve with herbed quinoa.

To make herbed quinoa, place quinoa in a small saucepan with the water, bring to the boil, then reduce the heat, cover and simmer for 10 minutes until all the water is absorbed. Melt the butter in a frying pan, add the herbs and cook for 1–2 minutes, stir in the cooked quinoa, season with salt and pepper and cook until heated through.

Serves 4

2 leeks
2 tbsp olive oil
4 half chicken breast fillets, skinned
2 cloves garlic, finely chopped
2 tbsp Dijon mustard
3/4 cup white wine
2 tbsp thyme leaves
salt and freshly ground pepper
3/4 cup cream

HERBED QUINOA
1½ cups quinoa, rinsed and drained
3 cups water
2 tbsp butter
2 tbsp fresh chives, chopped
2 tbsp flat-leaf parsley, chopped
1 tbsp fresh thyme leaves
salt and freshly cracked pepper

Chicken and Thyme Patties

½ cup red quinoa, rinsed and drained

1 cup water

1 kg (2 lb 4 oz) minced (ground) chicken

1 large onion, finely chopped

2 cloves garlic, finely chopped

1 tbsp Dijon mustard (or your favourite mustard)

2 tbsp fresh thyme leaves, finely chopped

1 tbsp fresh flat-leaf parsley, finely chopped

1 large egg

salt and freshly ground pepper

½ cup quinoa flakes

salt and freshly ground black pepper, extra

1 tbsp flat-leaf parsley, finely chopped, extra

Place quinoa in a small saucepan with the water, bring to the boil, then reduce heat, cover and simmer for 10–13 minutes until all the water is absorbed. Remove from heat and cool.

Place chicken in a large mixing bowl with the cooled quinoa, onion, garlic, mustard, thyme, parsley and egg, season with salt and pepper and mix well until thoroughly combined.

Mix the quinoa flakes with the extra parsley and season with a little salt and pepper.

Divide chicken mixture into 12 and shape into large patties then lightly press into the quinoa flake mixture to coat on both sides.

Heat oil in a large frying pan until hot and fry the patties on medium heat until golden brown on both sides and cooked right through.

Makes 12 patties

Tandoori Chicken

Cut chicken into strips. Mix with the yoghurt and tandoori paste and leave to marinade for at least half an hour, longer if possible.

Heat oil in a large, deep frying pan and brown chicken on high heat until it takes on some colour, about 8 minutes. Remove from heat.

Add onion to the pan and cook for 3–4 minutes until soft (you may need to add a little more oil to the pan). Stir in the garlic and cook for 30 seconds.

Add quinoa, stir well, return chicken to the pan then pour in stock or water and season with salt and pepper to taste.

Bring to the boil, reduce the heat, cover and simmer for 15 minutes. Stir in the beans and simmer for another 5 minutes.

Stir in coriander and serve with a good squeeze of lime juice, slices of red chilli and Greek yoghurt.

1 kg (2 lb 4 oz) chicken thigh fillets
1 tbsp Greek or natural yoghurt
3 tbsp tandoori paste
3 tbsp extra virgin olive oil
1 large brown onion, chopped
3 cloves garlic, finely chopped
1½ cups quinoa, rinsed and drained
3 cups hot chicken stock or water
salt and freshly ground black pepper
250 g (9 oz) green beans, cut into large
    pieces
handful of coriander (cilantro), roughly
    chopped
lime juice, for serving
red chilli, sliced, for garnish
Greek (natural) yoghurt, for serving

Serves 4

Baked 'Fried' Chicken

6 chicken thigh cutlets/chops,
  with skin on
1 cup buttermilk
salt and freshly ground black pepper
lemon juice, for serving

COATING
1 cup quinoa flour
1 tsp smoked paprika
1 tsp sweet paprika
1 tsp celery salt
1 tsp ground turmeric
½ tsp chilli powder
finely grated zest of 1 lemon
drizzle of olive oil

Buy even-sized chicken pieces. Make three incisions along each cutlet, cutting through the skin and a bit of the meat part.

Place into a bowl with the buttermilk and a little salt and pepper. Coat well, making sure you rub the buttermilk into each incision and the chicken is completely covered with it.

Leave to marinade in the fridge for at least 2–4 hours. The longer the better, even overnight is fine.

Preheat oven to 200°C (400°F) and line a baking tray with non-stick baking paper.

Make the coating by mixing the quinoa flour with the smoked and sweet paprika, celery salt, turmeric, chilli and lemon zest. Make sure all the spices are evenly distributed through the flour.

Give the chicken a little shake to remove any excess buttermilk, as you don't want it dripping in liquid, then coat completely with the coating mixture.

Continued ...

Place chicken on the baking tray and drizzle very lightly with a little olive oil, place in the oven and bake for 40–50 minutes until the chicken is cooked and golden brown.

Rest for 5 minutes loosely covered in foil, before serving with a squeeze of lemon juice. Delicious!

Serves 3–6

Note: Chicken thigh cutlets are also known as chicken chops and are the thigh with just one main thick bone left in them. They are great for use in dishes such as this one or in casseroles and curries as the thigh meat can take longer cooking times and the bone adds more flavour. You can use breast meat, drumsticks, whole chicken legs with a portion of the backbone attached, or wings if you prefer instead. I sometimes use a whole chicken, which I segment into pieces.

90

Stir-fried Chicken and Capsicums (Bell Peppers)

Place quinoa into a small saucepan with the water, bring to the boil, then reduce the heat, cover and simmer for 10 minutes until all the water is absorbed. Remove from heat and cool.

Heat oils in a wok until very hot, add the chicken and cook on high heat stirring constantly until the chicken is browned and almost cooked.

Add the onion, garlic, ginger, chillies and capsicums and continue cooking and stirring on high heat until the capsicums and onions begin to soften and colour, about 4–5 minutes.

Stir in the spring onions, soy and oyster sauce and a little water and cook for another 1–2 minutes.

Stir in the quinoa and cook until heated through, taste and adjust seasoning by adding some salt if you think necessary.

Serve garnished with extra chopped spring onions and chillies.

Serves 4–6

Note: I like to use olive oil in this dish; I use extra virgin olive oil in just about all my cooking. When using any Asian sauces or pastes, always check the ingredients as some ingredients used may be derived from wheat products and therefore contain wheat and gluten.

1½ cups quinoa, rinsed and drained

3 cups water

2 tbsp oil

1 tsp sesame oil

750 g (1 lb 10 oz) chicken breast fillets, cut into strips

1 onion, chopped into large pieces

3–4 cloves garlic, finely chopped

1 tbsp grated ginger

2 long green or red chillies, de-seeded and chopped

1 red capsicum (bell pepper), core removed and cut into chunks

1 green capsicum (bell pepper), core removed and cut into chunks

8 spring onions (scallions), sliced on the diagonal

2 tbsp tamari soy sauce

1 tbsp oyster sauce

¼–½ cup water

extra spring onions (scallions) and chillies, sliced, for garnish

Honey and Sesame Lemon Chicken

¾ cup quinoa flour

1 tsp Chinese five spice powder

1 tsp cracked black pepper

salt, to taste

1 egg

1 cup soda water

1 cup honey

juice of 1 lemon

1 tbsp sesame seeds

oil, for frying

1 kg (2 lb 4 oz) chicken breast tenderloins

½ cup quinoa flour, extra

Combine the flour, five spice powder, pepper and salt together.

Make a well in the centre, add the egg and slowly whisk in with the soda water and mix until you have a smooth batter mixture.

Place the honey, lemon juice and sesame seeds into a small saucepan and gently heat through until it comes to the boil. Continue to simmer on low heat for a few minutes until the sesame seeds just start to change colour. Remove from heat.

Meanwhile, start to heat the oil in a deep frying pan with enough oil to just come up half way the depth of the tenderloins.

Dredge the tenderloins in the extra flour then dip into the batter, making sure the chicken is completely covered. When the oil is hot, cook the tenderloins until golden on both sides.

Remove from the pan with a slotted spoon and drain on kitchen paper, keep warm until all the chicken is cooked.

When all the chicken is cooked place on a serving platter and drizzle the warmed honey sauce all over. Serve immediately.

Serves 4

Spicy Duck with Ginger and Chilli Quinoa

Make a marinade by mixing together the garlic, ginger, chilli, tamari, honey, oil, lime juice and zest, five spice powder and salt.

Make 2–3 cuts across the skin of each duck breast, cutting into the flesh, and rub all over with the marinade; make sure you get right into the cuts. Marinade for at least half an hour

Heat a large frying pan until hot, place the duck into the pan, skin side down, and cook until it is browned and the fat has rendered out.

Keep turning the duck and cook it for about 15 minutes for medium done or until it is cooked to your liking. Remove from the heat and cover with foil to rest. Or, after browning, you can finish cooking the duck in the oven if you prefer.

In the meantime, make the quinoa by heating the oil in a large frying pan. Add the garlic, chillies and ginger and sauté 1–2 minutes until soft. Stir in the spring onions and turmeric.

Mix in the quinoa and star anise then pour in the stock and season with salt.

Bring to the boil, reduce the heat, cover and simmer for 12–15 minutes until all the stock is absorbed. Garnish with extra sliced chillies and spring onions and serve with the duck and a good squeeze of lime juice.

Serves 4

1 clove garlic
1 tsp ground ginger
½–1 tsp chilli flakes
1 tbsp tamari soy sauce
1 tbsp honey
2 tsp olive oil
juice and zest of 1 lime
½ tsp five spice powder
salt, to taste
4 duck breasts, with the skins
lime, for serving

GINGER AND CHILLI QUINOA
2 tbsp olive oil
2 cloves garlic, grated
1–2 long red chillies, sliced or
    de-seeded and chopped
1 knob of ginger, peeled and thinly
    sliced
16 spring onions (scallions), sliced
    diagonally
½ tsp ground turmeric
1½ cups quinoa, rinsed and drained
2 star anise
3 cups hot chicken stock
salt, to taste
extra spring onions (scallions) and
    chillies, sliced, for garnish

Turkey Sausages

½ cup quinoa, rinsed and drained

1 cup water

500 g (17½ oz) minced (ground) turkey

2 cloves garlic, finely grated

1 small red onion, coarsely grated

4 spring onions (scallions), very finely
   sliced

1 long red chilli, de-seeded and finely
   chopped (optional)

1 tsp lemon zest

2 tsp dried mixed herbs

1 tsp sweet paprika

2 extra large eggs

salt and freshly ground black pepper

olive oil, for shallow cooking

lemon wedges, tomato sauce (ketchup)
   or mustard, for serving

Place quinoa in a small saucepan with the water, bring to the boil, then reduce heat, cover and simmer for 10 minutes until all the water is absorbed. Remove from the heat and cool.

Place turkey in a bowl with the garlic, onion, spring onions, chilli if using, lemon zest, mixed herbs, paprika and eggs, season with salt and pepper to taste.

Add the quinoa and mix really well to combine all of the ingredients together.

Take spoonfuls of the mixture and roll with your hands to form a sausage shape.

Heat a little olive oil in a large non-stick frying pan until hot.

Add the sausages and shallow-fry on a medium heat until cooked and browned all over.

Serve with lemon wedges or tomato or mustard sauce.

Makes about 18 sausages

Note: These turkey 'sausages' can be eaten hot or cold and are really nice for school lunches or picnics.

MEAT

Steak with Mushroom Gravy

Have the steak at room temperature and rub the oil, salt and pepper on both sides of the steak.

Heat a griddle pan or large frying pan until very hot.

Add the steak (you should hear an immediate sizzle) and cook for about 3–4 minutes on each side or to your liking, then turn over again and quickly cook for about 15–20 seconds only on both sides.

When the steak is cooked to your liking remove from the pan, place on to a plate and cover tightly with foil. Allow to rest for about 5–7 minutes.

While the steak is resting, pour a little oil in the pan add the mushrooms and garlic and quickly toss on high heat until the mushrooms collapse and take on some colour.

Stir in the flour then pour in the wine and deglaze the pan by allowing the alcohol to evaporate. Cook for about 1 minute.

Add the stock and parsley and season to taste. Cook for about 2–3 minutes until the mushrooms are cooked and the gravy has thickened.

Pour whatever juices have come out of the steaks while resting into the gravy and stir.

Serve the steaks with the mushroom gravy.

4 steaks, T-bone, rump, sirloin or fillet
extra virgin olive oil
salt and pepper

MUSHROOM GRAVY
250 g (4 oz) button mushrooms, finely sliced
extra virgin olive oil, extra
1–2 cloves garlic, finely chopped
2 tbsp quinoa flour
½ cup white wine
1 cup beef or chicken stock
2 tbsp flat-leaf parsley, finely chopped
salt and freshly cracked black pepper

Serves 4

Note: For a different take on the ever-popular steak and three vegetables meal why not serve this steak with the Three-Veg Bake on page 59.

Moroccan Lamb Roast with Yellow Quinoa

1 tbsp cumin seeds

1 tbsp coriander (cilantro) seeds

½ bunch fresh coriander (cilantro),
    including stems and root

4–5 large cloves garlic

1 tsp ground paprika

1 tsp ground cumin

1 tsp ground turmeric

½ tsp cinnamon

½–1 tsp dried chilli flakes

2 tbsp extra virgin olive oil

juice of 1 large lemon

salt

1 x 2 kg (4 lb 6 oz) boned leg of lamb

Greek yoghurt, for serving

lemon juice, for serving

coriander (cilantro) leaves, for serving

Dry-roast the cumin and coriander seeds in a small non-stick frying pan until fragrant. Keep an eye on them as they can burn very easily.

Place seeds in a mortar and pestle and grind to a coarse powder.

Chop the coriander root and stems into small pieces, add to the mortar and pestle with the garlic, paprika, cumin, turmeric, cinnamon and chilli and grind to a paste with the olive oil and lemon juice.

Finely chop the coriander leaves and mix into the paste, season with salt.

Lay out the lamb onto a large roasting pan that has been lined with non-stick baking paper (this helps with the washing up later). Using a sharp knife, make some deep cuts all along the inside part of the lamb so as to open it up even more, known as a 'butterfly' cut. This not only helps the marinade penetrate the meat more but also cuts down on the cooking time.

Completely cover the lamb all over with the marinade making sure you rub it right into all the cuts. Cover and leave to marinade in the fridge for at least 4–6 hours or, preferably, overnight.

Take the lamb out of the fridge 1 hour before cooking and bring back to room temperature.

Continued ...

Preheat oven to 200°C (400°F) and roast the lamb for 1–1¼ hours, depending on how well done you like your lamb to be cooked. Lamb is best cooked when still slightly pink in the centre.

Remove from the oven, cover tightly with foil and rest for a good 10–15 minutes before serving with the yellow quinoa.

While the lamb is cooking, prepare the yellow quinoa. Heat oil in a large, deep frying pan and cook the mustard seeds until they start to pop. Add the spring onions and sauté until they are soft.

Add the cardamom, turmeric and cinnamon and cook for about 1 minute. Stir in the quinoa, season with salt and water then pour in the water, bring back to the boil, reduce the heat to low cover and simmer for about 15 minutes until all the liquid is absorbed.

Fluff up with a fork and serve on a large platter topped with the sliced lamb. Squeeze some extra lemon over the lamb and sprinkle with extra coriander leaves.

Serve with a dollop of Greek yoghurt.

Serves 6

Note: This is a family favourite in my house and is a great meal to prepare when you have guests. The cooking time for the lamb varies according to your oven but also depends on how you like your lamb.

YELLOW QUINOA
1–2 tbsp extra virgin olive oil
1 tsp black mustard seeds
6 spring onions (scallions), sliced
7 cardamom pods
1 heaped tbsp grated fresh turmeric or
   2 tsp ground
¼ tsp cinnamon
2 cups quinoa, rinsed and drained
salt and freshly cracked black pepper
4 cups boiling water

Chilli Con Carne

2 tbsp olive oil

1 large onion, finely chopped

500 g (17½ oz) minced (ground) beef

3 cloves garlic, chopped

2 tbsp dried oregano

2 tbsp ground cumin

1 tbsp ground paprika

½–1 tsp chilli powder

2 tbsp tomato paste (concentrate)

2 x 400 g (14 oz) cans diced tomatoes

salt, to taste

1 cup water

1½ cups, quinoa, rinsed and drained

2½ cups boiling water

2 x 400 g (14 oz) cans red kidney beans, drained and rinsed

parmesan, grated, for serving

coriander (cilantro), chopped, for garnish

sour cream, for garnish

avocado, sliced (optional)

Heat oil in a large, deep frying pan and sauté onion until soft and golden. Add the beef and continue cooking until browned, making sure any lumps are broken up.

Stir in the garlic and cook for about 30 seconds until fragrant then add the oregano, cumin, paprika and chilli and cook for about 1 minute,

Stir in tomato paste then add the undrained tomatoes, salt and water. Reduce heat, cover and simmer on low heat for about 15 minutes.

Stir in the quinoa and boiling water, cover and simmer for about 20 minutes, stirring occasionally until the quinoa is cooked.

Stir in the red kidney beans and simmer on low heat until the beans are heated through and all the flavours have combined (about 5 minutes).

Rest for about 10 minutes before serving with a sprinkling of grated parmesan, some fresh coriander and a dollop of sour cream. Slices of fresh avocado are also lovely served with this chilli.

Serves 6

quinoa for families

Beef with Black Bean Sauce

Place quinoa in a small saucepan with the stock and star anise, bring to the boil, then reduce the heat, cover and simmer for 10–12 minutes until all the stock is absorbed. Remove from heat and keep warm.

Meanwhile, combine the steak in a bowl with the flour and the soy sauce.

Heat oil until really hot in a wok or a large frying pan, add the meat and any juices from the bowl and cook on high heat until browned, stirring regularly. Remove from wok.

Heat a little more oil in wok; add the capsicums and sauté on high heat for about 2–3 minutes. Then add the spring onions and garlic and sauté for another 1–2 minutes.

Stir in the black bean paste and oyster sauce. Return the meat to the wok with any of its juices and toss well to combine. Pour in the water and keep tossing constantly until mixture starts to boil and thicken.

Rest for about 5 minutes before serving with the quinoa. Remove and discard the star anise from the quinoa before serving.

1½ cups quinoa, rinsed and drained
3 cups chicken stock
2 star anise
750 g (1 lb 12½ oz) rump or fillet steak, sliced into thin strips
1 tbsp quinoa flour
2 tbsp soy sauce
2–3 tbsp oil
oil, extra
1 red capsicum (bell pepper), cut into strips
1 green capsicum (bell pepper), cut into strips
6 spring onion (scallions), sliced into 2.5 cm (1 in) pieces
3 cloves garlic, finely chopped
2–3 tbsp black bean paste
1 tbsp oyster sauce
½–¾ cup water

Serves 4

Note: When using any Asian sauces or pastes such as the black bean paste, soy and oyster sauce, always check the ingredients as some ingredients used may be derived from wheat products and therefore contain wheat and gluten.

Parsley, Garlic and Lemon-crusted Lamb

Preheat oven to 200°C (400°F) and line a baking tray with non-stick baking paper

Place parsley, garlic, lemon zest, juice and oil in a food processor and process using the pulse setting until all the ingredients are finely chopped.

Add the quinoa flakes, salt and pepper and process for a few seconds until everything is combined and resembles a paste.

Trim lamb of any excess fat and place on the baking tray, rub with a little extra virgin olive oil and season with salt and pepper. Place in the oven and roast for 10 minutes only.

After 10 minutes, remove lamb from oven and coat with the parsley mixture pressing it down firmly.

Return lamb to the oven and roast for about 20 minutes until the lamb is cooked medium-well and the topping is golden. Lamb should be slightly pink inside but adjust cooking time as per your preference.

Remove from the oven, cover with foil, and leave to rest for a good 10 minutes before slicing and serving.

Serves 4

Note: The number of cutlets you prepare and serve is up to you. I usually like to serve three to four cutlets per person depending on the appetites at the table.

2 cups parsley, chopped
3 cloves garlic
zest of 2 lemons
2 tbsp lemon juice
1 tsp extra virgin olive oil
1 cup quinoa flakes
salt and freshly cracked pepper
2 racks of lamb made up of
    6–8 frenched lamb cutlets each
extra virgin olive oil, extra
salt and freshly cracked black pepper,
    extra

Sage-crumbed Pork Cutlets with Apple Sauce

4 pork cutlets

1½ cups quinoa flakes

1½–2 tbsp fresh sage, finely chopped

2 tbsp chives, finely chopped

1 tsp ground sweet paprika

salt and freshly cracked black pepper

2 eggs

1 tbsp milk

1 tbsp English mustard

⅓ cup quinoa flour

olive oil

APPLE SAUCE

2 Granny Smith apples, peeled, cored and cut into chunks

1–2 tbsp brown sugar

½ cup water

Using a meat mallet or rolling pin, pound the pork cutlets until they are about 1 cm (½ in) thick.

Combine the quinoa flakes with the sage, chives, paprika and season with salt and pepper.

Whisk the eggs with the milk and mustard.

Dust the chops with the flour, dip into the egg then press into the flake mixture to coat evenly. If time permits, rest meat after coating in the refrigerator for 30 minutes or so.

Heat oil in a large frying pan and shallow-fry the cutlets until golden and cooked on both sides.

To make the apple sauce, place the apples, sugar and water in a small saucepan and bring to the boil. Reduce heat and simmer, covered, until apples are soft. Mash with a fork. If apples dry out before they are cooked, add a little more water.

Serve cutlets with sauce.

Serves 4

Ham, Leek and Cheese Pie

1 tbsp olive oil
1 large leek, sliced (including the tender
   green parts)
150 g (5 oz) ham, sliced or chopped
2 cloves garlic, finely chopped
1 tbsp horseradish cream
6 large eggs
300 ml (10¼ fl oz) cream
300 ml (10¼ fl oz) full-cream milk
²/₃ cup quinoa flour
¾ tsp gluten-free baking powder
1 cup tasty or mild cheddar cheese,
   grated
salt and freshly cracked pepper

Preheat oven to 180°C (350°F) and lightly grease an oven-proof baking dish.

Heat oil in a frying pan and sauté leek for 3–4 minutes until soft and golden then add the ham and continue cooking for another 2–3 minutes. Stir in the garlic then remove from heat and stir in the horseradish cream.

In a bowl, whisk the eggs with the cream and milk until well combined. Sift the flour and the baking powder together then stir into the egg mixture with the cheese and season with salt and pepper.

Place the ham and leeks into the prepared baking dish then pour over the egg mixture, give it a little stir and sprinkle with a little more pepper. Bake for 40–50 minutes or until the pie is set and golden.

Rest for at least 10 minutes before cutting and serving.

Serves 4

Meat Pie

2 cups quinoa flour

½ tsp salt

1 tsp baking powder

125 g (4 oz) very cold unsalted butter,
      cut into pieces

½ cup icy cold water

1 egg, beaten

tomato sauce, for serving

FILLING

1 tbsp olive oil

1 large onion, chopped

450 g (16 oz) minced (ground) beef

2 cloves garlic, finely chopped

1 tbsp tomato paste (concentrate)

1 tsp mixed herbs

1 tbsp quinoa flour

salt and freshly cracked pepper

1 cup beef stock

1 tbsp of your favourite chutney

Place the flour, salt and baking powder in a food processor. Pulse for a few seconds to aerate the flour then add the butter and pulse until the mixture resembles fine breadcrumbs.

With the motor running, add the water a little at a time until the dough comes together and turns into a ball.

Turn onto a floured surface and shape into a flat disc. Wrap in plastic wrap and refrigerate for about 1 hour.

To make the filling, heat the oil in a frying pan or saucepan and sauté onion until golden. Add the beef and cook until browned then stir in the garlic and tomato paste and cook for about 1 minute.

Stir in the herbs and the flour, season with salt and pepper then add the stock. Bring to the boil, lower heat and simmer covered for about 5 minutes. Remove from the heat, stir in the chutney and allow to cool.

Preheat the oven to 180°C (350°F) and lightly oil four 125 ml (4 oz) individual pie tins.

Divide the pastry into four then place onto a sheet of non-stick baking paper. Cut each piece into two pieces, one to cover the base and sides of the pie tin and the other (a smaller piece) to use as a lid. Roll out the pastry and line the tins.

Continued ...

Divide the filling between the four pie tins. Cover the pies with a pastry lid then lightly press the edges together to seal. Cut a small vent on the top of each pie.

If you're feeling up to it, cut out some decorative shapes from any leftover pastry for the tops of the pies. Brush with beaten egg and bake for about 25-30 minutes until golden. Stand for about 10 minutes before gently removing from tins. Serve with lots of tomato sauce.

Makes 4 pies

Note: These pies may sound a bit fiddly to make but they are actually very easy. Keep in mind that because quinoa flour is used to make the pastry, it may not roll out as easily as pastry made with regular flour and you may need to ease the pastry into the tins. This is why I find the pastry is much easier to handle and to transfer into the tins after rolling onto non-stick paper first. After you have made them for the first time you will see they are not hard at all to make and are really worth the little extra time.

Sweet Potato, Bacon and Chilli Bake

Preheat oven to 180°C (350°F) and lightly grease a 30 x 20 cm (8 x 10 in) baking dish.

Place quinoa in a small saucepan with the water, bring to the boil, then reduce the heat, cover and simmer for about 10 minutes until all the water is absorbed. Remove from the heat and cool.

Place the quinoa in a large bowl with the potato, bacon, spring onions, chilli, garlic, turmeric, eggs, cheese, salt and pepper and mix well to combine.

Pour mixture into baking dish and bake for 45–50 minutes until golden and crisp. Rest for around 10 minutes before slicing.

Serves 6

Note: This can be eaten hot or cold and it is ideal for lunches or to take to picnics. It is best to grate the potato just before you use it as it can discolour very quickly.

¾ cup quinoa, rinsed and drained

1½ cups water

500 g (17½ oz) sweet potato, peeled and coarsely grated

3–4 rashers bacon, rind removed, and chopped

4 spring onions (scallions), sliced

1 long red chilli, de-seeded and finely chopped

2 cloves garlic, finely chopped

1 tsp ground turmeric

4 eggs

1½ cups tasty or mild cheddar cheese, grated

salt and freshly ground pepper

Chorizo Sausage with Caramelised Onions and Smoked Paprika

1½ cups quinoa, rinsed and drained

3 cups water

4 chorizo sausages, thickly sliced

1 tbsp extra virgin olive oil

2 large onions, halved then sliced

2 cloves garlic, chopped

½–1 tsp chilli flakes

2 tsp smoked paprika

1½ cups frozen peas

¼ cup water

salt and freshly cracked black pepper

2 tbsp parsley, chopped, for serving

Place quinoa in a small to medium saucepan with the water, bring to the boil, then reduce the heat, cover and simmer for 10 minutes or until all the water is absorbed. Remove from heat.

Sauté chorizo in a large, non-stick frying pan until lightly browned (there is no need to add any oil to the pan at this stage as the chorizo should render some of its own fat).

Remove the chorizo from pan with a slotted spoon and set aside.

Add the oil to the pan if necessary and cook onion, stirring regularly until soft and caramelised, for about 5 minutes, stir in the garlic and chilli flakes and cook for about 30 seconds then stir in the chilli and paprika.

Add the frozen peas and water and cook for about 4-5 minutes, stirring frequently until peas have thawed and are just cooked.

Stir in the quinoa and the chorizo sausage, season with salt and pepper and cook for another 3-4 minutes until heated through. Sprinkle with parsley and serve.

Serves 4

SEAFOOD

Salmon with Fennel and Tomatoes

Preheat oven to 200°C (400°F) and line a baking tray with non-stick baking paper.

Make two to three incisions across each piece of salmon and rub in the mustard then sprinkle with lemon juice.

Place the salmon, skin side up, onto the baking tray and add the tomatoes. Season salmon and tomatoes with salt and pepper and drizzle with olive oil.

Bake for 15–18 minutes until salmon is cooked and tomatoes have collapsed. Remove from the oven, cool and flake the salmon into chunks with or without the skin.

In the meantime, heat oil in a large frying pan and sauté onion until lightly browned. Stir in the garlic and mustard seeds and cook for 1–2 minutes.

Add the fennel and cook for 4–5 minutes until soft, then stir in the mustard.

Stir in the dill, quinoa and water and season with salt and pepper. Bring to the boil, reduce the heat, cover and simmer for about 15 minutes until the quinoa is cooked and all the liquid is absorbed.

Gently toss the salmon and tomatoes through the quinoa, squeeze a good amount of lemon juice over the top and garnish with extra chopped dill.

750 g (1 lb 10 oz) fresh salmon
1 tbsp Dijon mustard
1–2 tbsp lemon juice
250 g (9 oz) grape or cherry tomatoes
salt and freshly cracked pepper
1 tbsp extra virgin olive oil
2 tbsp extra virgin olive oil
1 red onion, chopped
2 cloves garlic, chopped
1 tsp mustard seeds
1 large fennel bulb, trimmed and sliced
1 tbsp Dijon mustard, extra
½ cup fresh dill, chopped
1½ cups quinoa, rinsed and drained
3 cups hot water
salt and freshly cracked black pepper
2 tbsp lemon juice
dill, chopped, for garnish

Serves 4–6

seafood

Smoked Cod Kedgeree

1½ cups quinoa

3 cups water

750 g (1 lb 10 oz) smoked cod

3 hard-boiled eggs

1 tbsp butter

2 tbsp extra virgin olive oil

6 spring onions (scallions), sliced

1 long red chilli, sliced

2 tsp curry paste or powder

salt and freshly ground black pepper

½ cup finely chopped flat-leaf parsley

lemon juice, for serving

parsley, chopped, for serving

Place quinoa in a small saucepan with the water, bring to the boil, then reduce the heat, cover and simmer for 10 minutes until all the water is absorbed. Remove from heat and cool completely.

Place the cod in a large frying pan with just enough water to cover. Bring to a simmering point, and then simmer, uncovered, for about 10 minutes until the fish is tender. Drain and reserve about 2 tablespoons of the cooking liquid.

Remove and discard the skin and any bones from the fish and flake the flesh into large pieces/ Peel and chop two of the eggs and slice the third.

Melt the butter and heat the oil in a large frying pan, add the spring onions and chilli and cook for 2–3 minutes until tender. Stir in the curry paste and reserved liquid and cook for 1–2 minutes.

Stir through the quinoa, coating completely in the curry. Add the fish and chopped egg, season with salt and pepper and gently toss to combine everything.

Cook for about 3–5 minutes over gentle heat until heated through then stir in the parsley.

Place onto a serving platter, sprinkle with lemon juice and serve garnished with the sliced egg and extra parsley.

Serves 4

Note: You can substitute the cod with fresh salmon. Poach the salmon as you would the cod.

quinoa for families

Fried 'Rice'

Place quinoa in a small saucepan with the water, bring to the boil, then reduce the heat, cover and simmer for 10 minutes until all the water is absorbed. Remove from heat and spread out onto a tray to cool and dry out completely.

Lightly whisk the eggs with the soy sauce and water. Heat the oil in a wok until hot, add the beaten eggs and swirl around to form an omelette.

When the eggs have set, tilt wok away from you and, using a spatula, carefully roll up the omelette. Remove from the wok and slice into thin strips and set aside.

Heat extra oil and sesame oil in the wok, add the bacon, prawns and spring onions including as much of the green part as is usable. Cook on high heat, stirring constantly, until the prawns change colour and the bacon starts to crisp up.

Add the peas and corn spears and continue stirring for 2–3 minutes.

Stir in the soy sauce and the cooled quinoa and continue cooking for 3–4 minutes until quinoa is heated through. Gently stir in the egg strips and serve with an extra drizzle of soy sauce and chopped spring onions.

1½ cups quinoa, rinsed and drained
3 cups water
1 tbsp oil
2 eggs
1 tsp soy sauce
1 tbsp water
2 tbsp oil extra
½ tsp sesame oil
3 rashers bacon, rind removed and diced
500 g (17½ oz) green prawns, peeled and de-veined
8 spring onions (scallions), sliced
½ cup frozen peas
200 g (7 oz) fresh baby corn spears or 1 x 400 g (14 oz) canned, drained
2–3 tbsp light tamari soy sauce
soy sauce, for serving
spring onions (scallions), chopped, for serving

Serves 6

Note: This is a family favourite in our house; it is just so much lighter to digest than the usual fried rice.

Tuna Mornay with a Crunchy Topping

1 x 425 g (14½ oz) canned tuna in brine
  or spring water
30 g (1 oz) butter
3 tbsp quinoa flour
1 tsp curry powder
1¼ cups milk
salt and pepper
½–¾ cup tasty or mild cheddar cheese,
  grated
3 cups cornflakes
1 cup tasty or mild cheddar cheese,
  grated, extra
1 tsp butter

Preheat oven to 180°C (350°F).

Drain and flake the tuna and place into a medium casserole dish.

Melt butter in a saucepan then stir in the flour and curry powder to form a roux.

Slowly pour in the milk, stirring constantly until sauce starts to thicken and bubble.

Season with salt and pepper then stir in the cheese and cook for about 2 minutes until cheese has melted into the sauce and the sauce is thick and bubbly.

Pour sauce over tuna and mix thoroughly to combine.

In a separate bowl, lightly crush the cornflakes and mix with the extra cheese and sprinkle over tuna.

Dot with a little butter and place in the oven to bake for about 15–20 minutes or until topping is golden and crispy.

Serves 4

Note: This has been a family favourite for years. I used to use regular flour but swapped over to quinoa flour when I discovered it. It works just as well and you can't tell the difference at all. Everyone I have served this to absolutely loves it.

Prawn (Shrimp) Cutlets

Peel and de-vein prawns leaving tail intact and butterfly them (see below).

Mix together the quinoa flakes, paprika, lemon zest, salt and pepper.

Coat the prawns in the flake mixture, pressing down to make sure they are well coated and the coating sticks to the prawns.

Heat enough oil on medium heat in a large frying pan until hot. There should be enough oil to just come up about halfway up the prawns.

Add the prawns and shallow-fry until golden on both sides and the prawns are cooked.

Sprinkle with lemon juice and serve.

Serves 4

Note: To butterfly prawns first peel them. After peeling the prawns make a cut deep into the back of each one without cutting right through, remove the vein then gently flatten the prawn. What you should be left with is a prawn that has been almost sliced in half and opened like a book with the tail intact.

I have allowed six prawns per person and I like to use quite large prawns as they tend to shrink during cooking. You might like to vary the amount according to your diners' appetites.

24 extra large green prawns (shrimp)
1½ cups quinoa flakes
1 tsp ground paprika
zest of 1 lemon
salt and freshly cracked pepper
olive oil, for frying
lemon juice, for serving

Curried Prawns (Shrimp) with Toasted Coconut Quinoa

2 tbsp olive oil

2 medium onions, halved then sliced

3 cloves garlic, finely chopped

2 tbsp curry powder

1 tsp ground cumin

2 tbsp tamari soy sauce

2–3 medium carrots, sliced

salt and freshly cracked pepper

1½ cups water or fish stock

1 kg (2 lb 4 oz) peeled green prawns (shrimp)

1½ cups frozen peas

lemon juice, for serving

TOASTED COCONUT QUINOA

2 cups quinoa, rinsed and drained

2½ cups water

1 x 400 g (14 oz) can coconut milk

1 cup coconut flakes, shredded

Heat oil in a large saucepan and sauté onion on medium heat until soft and lightly browned. Add the garlic and cook for about 1 minute.

Stir in the curry powder and cumin and cook for another minute, then add the soy sauce and carrots. Season with salt and pepper then pour in the water or stock. Stir the pan, making sure to scrap the bottom of the pan, to release all the flavours that have developed.

Bring to the boil then reduce the heat, cover and simmer for about 10 minutes.

Add the prawns, bring back to the boil then reduce the heat, cover and simmer on low heat for another 10 minutes or until the prawns are cooked. Stir in the peas and simmer for 5 minutes more. Serve over a bed of toasted coconut quinoa with some lemon juice squeezed over.

To make the toasted coconut quinoa, place the quinoa in a medium saucepan with the water and coconut milk, bring to the boil, then reduce the heat, cover and simmer for 12–15 minutes until all the liquid is absorbed.

Dry-roast the coconut flakes in a small, non-stick frying pan, turning and tossing regularly so it doesn't burn until it is a light golden colour. Using a fork, toss the toasted coconut through the quinoa and serve with the curried prawns.

Serves 4

Moroccan-style Baked Fish

Preheat oven to 190°C (375°F)

Heat the oil in a medium-sized frying pan and sauté the spring onions until they start to change colour. Add the garlic and cook for about 30 seconds until fragrant.

Stir in the ground coriander and coriander seeds, ground cumin and cumin seeds, paprika, chilli and ginger and cook for about 1 minute. Add a little more oil if mixture is too dry and starting to burn.

Add the lemon juice, zest, parsley, fresh coriander, water and quinoa flakes and season with salt and pepper. Stir and cook for about 1–2 minutes until the herbs collapse and the quinoa has mixed in with all the other flavours and the mixture resembles a moist paste. Remove from heat.

Place fish onto a greased, shallow baking dish and season with salt and pepper. Cover each piece of fish with evenly divided quinoa mixture and drizzle with extra virgin olive oil and a squeeze of lemon juice. Cover with foil and bake for about 15 minutes then remove the foil and bake for a further 10 minutes or so until fish is cooked.

Drizzle with extra virgin olive oil and a good squeeze of lemon juice to serve.

3 tbsp extra virgin olive oil
6 spring onions (scallions), sliced
3 cloves garlic, finely chopped
½ tsp ground coriander (cilantro)
1 tsp coriander (cilantro) seeds, left whole
1 tsp ground cumin
½ tsp cumin seeds, left whole
1 tsp sweet paprika
½ tsp chilli flakes
1 tsp ground ginger
juice and zest of 1 lemon
½ bunch flat-leaf parsley, very finely chopped
½ bunch fresh coriander (cilantro), including roots and stems, very finely chopped
⅔ cup water
1 cup quinoa flakes
salt and freshly ground black pepper
extra virgin olive oil, extra
lemon juice, extra
4 largish snapper steaks
extra virgin olive oil, for serving
lemon juice, for serving

Serves 4

Note: You can also prepare a whole fish using this method, just use part of the mixture inside the fish and cover the outside with the remainder.

seafood

Seafood Paella

4 tbsp extra virgin olive oil

1 large onion, finely chopped

1 large red capsicum, seeded and
  chopped

4 cloves garlic, finely chopped

2 cups quinoa, rinsed and drained

1 x 400 g (14 oz) tin diced tomatoes

500 g (17½ oz) calamari tubes, sliced

3½ cups fish or chicken stock

1 tsp saffron strands

sea salt and ground black pepper

750 g (1 lb 10 oz) large green prawns,
  unpeeled

750 g (1 lb 10 oz) mussels, scrubbed

1 cup frozen peas

flat-leaf parsley, chopped

lemon wedges, for garnish

Heat olive oil in a large, deep frying pan or a paella dish if you have one and sauté onion and capsicum until onion is soft and golden.

Stir in garlic and quinoa then pour in tomatoes, sliced calamari, stock and saffron, season with salt and pepper, cover loosely with lid or foil and cook for about 12 minutes.

Arrange prawns and mussels on top then cover again and cook for another 10 minutes, adding more stock if necessary but only if the pan is completely dry.

Gently stir in the peas and cook, covered, for another 5-10 minutes until quinoa is cooked.

Sprinkle with parsley and a good squeeze of lemon juice. Serve with lemon wedges arranged on top.

Serves 6-8

Note: Traditionally, a proper paella is supposed to have a slightly burnt and crunchy crust at the bottom of the pan which everyone fights over as it is considered to be the best part. The amount of cooking time above is usually sufficient to cook the seafood and quinoa completely but to also allow for a crunchy base to develop. You can use whatever combination of seafood you prefer. You will need a pan or paella pan that has a large cooking surface to get the best results when cooking this dish but to also accommodate all the seafood and other ingredients.

Sushi

Place quinoa in a small saucepan with the water, bring to the boil, then reduce the heat, cover and simmer for 15 minutes until all the water is absorbed. The quinoa is cooked for a little longer in this dish as it needs to be a little gluggy.

Remove from the heat, stir in the sugar and vinegar and mix well—the quinoa should be quite sticky. Cool it a little.

Place the nori seaweed sheet, shiny side down, on a bamboo rolling mat.

Divide the quinoa into four and, using wet fingertips, spread evenly over the nori sheet leaving a 2½ cm (1 in) border at the end.

Dab a small amount of wasabi along the quinoa in a straight line at the edge closest to you. Place the fillings of your choice on top of the wasabi in a neat line.

Lift the bamboo mat at the closest edge to you and begin to slowly and tightly roll the nori sheet, at the same time separating the bamboo mat away from the rolled part of the nori sheet. Lightly wet the end of the sheet and gently press to join the edge together.

Using a wet serrated knife, slice the sushi in half or in 5-6 pieces.

1 cup quinoa, rinsed and drained
2½ cups water
1½ tbsp sugar
2 tbsp rice wine vinegar
4 nori sheets
wasabi paste
choice of fillings: fresh or tinned tuna, crab, prawns, fresh salmon, cooked chicken, strips of cucumber, carrot, avocado, spring onions (scallions), capsicum (bell pepper)

Makes 4 large sushi rolls

Note: I find that white quinoa works best in this recipe.

135

seafood

SWEET THINGS

Sticky Date Puddings with Caramel Sauce

500 g (17½ oz) dried dates
2½ cups water
1 tsp bicarbonate of soda (baking soda)
250 g (9 oz) unsalted butter
1¼ cups caster (superfine) sugar
4 extra large eggs
2 tsp vanilla extract
1 tsp ground cinnamon
2 cups quinoa flour
2 tsp baking powder
strawberries, for garnish

CARAMEL SAUCE
200 g (7 oz) unsalted butter
2 cups brown sugar
1 cup pouring cream
1 tsp vanilla extract

Place dates and water into a medium to large saucepan and bring slowly to the boil, reduce the heat and simmer for 1 minute.

Remove from the heat, stir in the bicarbonate of soda and set aside to cool completely.

The whole mixture will froth up when you add the soda so make sure you use a big enough saucepan so it doesn't spill over and don't worry about all the liquid left as the date mixture will thicken as it cools.

Preheat oven to 160°C (325°F) and grease 12 1-cup capacity tin moulds

Using electric beaters, cream the butter and sugar together until light. Beat in the eggs, one at a time, with the vanilla and cinnamon.

Sift the flour and baking powder and slowly incorporate with the creamed butter mixture. Fold in the cooled dates and divide cake mixture evenly between the prepared tins.

Continued ...

Place tins on a baking tray and bake for
35–40 minutes. When cooled, run a thin knife
along the side of the moulds to loosen the
puddings, then invert onto a serving plate and
serve with lots of caramel sauce and a fanned
strawberry.

To make the caramel sauce, place all ingredients
into a small saucepan and simmer for a few
minutes until the sauce starts to bubble and
thicken.

Makes 12 individual puddings

Note: I prefer to make this recipe as little individual
puddings—they are a nice serving size—and have
always done so as I like the look of them when
served. Also they cook a lot quicker. You can, of
course, make one large pudding if you prefer, just
vary the cooking time.

Grandma's Lemon Delicious

⅓ cup quinoa flour

1 tsp baking powder

½ tsp bicarbonate of soda (baking soda)

60 g (2 oz) butter

½ cup caster (superfine) sugar

juice and rind of 2 lemons

2 extra large eggs, separated

1 cup milk

icing (confectioners') sugar, for dusting

Preheat oven to 180°C (350°F) and grease a deep six-cup capacity ovenproof dish with butter.

Sift together the flour, baking powder and bicarbonate soda and set aside.

Cream the butter, sugar and lemon rind together. Beat in the egg yolks and mix until light and fluffy.

Fold in the flour alternatively with the milk and then stir in the lemon juice. Beat the egg whites with electric beaters until stiff then fold lightly into the flour mixture. Don't be too concerned if the mixture looks curdled at any stage, it will sort itself out during cooking.

Pour the mixture into the prepared dish and stand in another dish with enough hot water to come up halfway up the dish with the cake batter.

Bake for approximately 35-40 minutes until golden on the top and firm.

Remove from the oven and the water bath and stand for five minutes before serving, dusted with icing sugar. This dessert is best served warm.

Serves 4

Note: This is my mother-in-law's recipe and I remember she used to prepare it for her husband on a regular basis. I now make it with quinoa flour, which I find makes a lighter pudding. This recipe is best made just before serving.

High-protein Smoothie

Soak the quinoa flakes in the water for about
5 minutes until all the water is absorbed.

Place in a blender with the strawberries, honey,
vanilla, egg whites, milk and ice cubes. Blend until
smooth. Serve immediately.

Variations: You can add low-fat yoghurt to the above
and you can substitute the strawberries with:
2 tsp instant coffee and ¼ tsp cinnamon
OR
2 ripe bananas
OR
a combination of strawberries and bananas.

Serves 2

Note: This is a great drink to start the day with,
especially if you don't have time for the conventional
sit-down breakfast.

3 tbsp quinoa flakes
5 tbsp cold water
1 cup fresh strawberries
1–2 tbsp honey
2 tsp vanilla extract
2 egg whites
2 cups fat-reduced milk
ice cubes

143

sweet things

Steamed Christmas Fruit Pudding

½ cup quinoa flour

½ tsp bicarbonate of soda (baking soda)

½ tsp gluten-free baking powder

1 heaped tsp ground cinnamon

2 tsp mixed spice

pinch of salt

¾ cup quinoa flakes

1 cup brown sugar, tightly packed

675 g (23½ oz) mixed fruit

50 g (1¾ oz) mixed peel

50 g (1¾ oz) flaked almonds, chopped

grated zest of 1 lemon

grated zest of 1 orange

3 tbsp orange juice

2 tbsp treacle

2–3 tbsp brandy

2 extra large eggs, lightly beaten

125 g (4 oz) butter, melted

Grease an 8–10 cup pudding basin with butter.

Sift together the flour, bicarbonate of soda, baking powder, cinnamon, mixed spice and salt.

Mix in the quinoa flakes, sugar, mixed fruit (break up any lumps of fruit that may have stuck together), mixed peel, almonds, lemon and orange zest, orange juice, treacle and brandy. Add the eggs and butter and stir well until evenly mixed.

Pour mixture into the prepared basin, pushing down well into the basin and flatten the top with the back of a spoon.

Loosely cover the top of the pudding with a sheet of non-stick baking paper then cover the top of the basin with plastic wrap. Secure by using an elastic band to hold the plastic wrap in place.

Fill a large saucepan with enough hot water to come halfway up the side of the pudding basin and carefully place the pudding into the saucepan.

Reduce heat to a low simmer, cover saucepan with a lid and cook pudding for about 3 hours. Remove from the saucepan and allow to cool in the pudding basin.

Gently run a thin knife along the inside of the basin to release the pudding then invert on to serving platter and serve with brandy custard. You can serve the pudding cold or warm by re-heating in microwave. It can be prepared up to 4–6 weeks before serving.

Serves 8

Carrot Cake with Cream Cheese Frosting

Preheat oven to 160°C (325°F) and grease a 24 cm (9½ in) non-stick, square tin.

Sift together the flour, bicarbonate, baking powder, cinnamon and salt.

Using electric beaters, beat the eggs, sugar and vanilla until light and fluffy then mix in the oil.

Stir in the dry ingredients then fold in the carrot and walnuts.

Pour into the prepared tin and bake for about 45 minutes or until a skewer comes out clean when tested.

Remove from oven and cool in the tin for about 15 minutes then turn out onto a wire rack to cool completely.

When cooled, ice the top of the cake with cream cheese frosting, decorate with extra walnuts and sprinkle with cinnamon powder. I like to refrigerate the cake after icing for about half an hour to allow the icing to set.

To make the frosting, using an electric mixer, combine cream cheese, butter, icing sugar and vanilla. Beat until light and fluffy.

Serves 8–10

1⅓ cup quinoa flour

1½ tsp bicarbonate of soda (baking soda)

1½ tsp gluten-free baking powder

1½ tsp ground cinnamon

pinch of salt

3 extra large eggs

1 cup caster (superfine) sugar

2 tsp vanilla extract

¾ cup extra light olive oil or vegetable oil

2 cups raw carrot, grated

½ cup walnuts, finely chopped

walnut halves, for decoration

ground cinnamon, for decoration

CREAM CHEESE FROSTING

125 g (4 oz) cream cheese, at room temperature

3 tbsp butter, softened

250 g (9 oz) pure icing (confectioners') sugar, sifted

1½ tsp vanilla extract

149

Tiramisu

2 tbsp instant coffee

2 tbsp boiling water

1½ cups quinoa flour

1½ tsp gluten-free baking powder

1½ tsp bicarbonate of soda (baking soda)

1 tbsp cocoa powder

125 g (4 oz) butter, softened

2 tsp vanilla extract

1 cup caster (superfine) sugar

2 extra large eggs

⅓ cup milk

FILLING

500 g (17½ oz) mascarpone cheese

3-4 tbsp icing (confectioners') sugar

2 tsp vanilla extract

zest and juice of 1 large orange

½ cup milk

1 x 670 g (23½ oz) jar of cherries in
    syrup

cocoa powder, for garnish

chocolate shavings, for garnish

1 quantity coffee cake

To make the coffee cake, preheat the oven to 160°C (325°F) and grease a 20 cm (8 in) non-stick square cake tin.

Dissolve the coffee in the boiling water and set aside. Sift quinoa flour, baking powder, bicarbonate of soda and cocoa together.

Cream butter, vanilla and sugar together until creamy, add the eggs one at a time and beat until light and fluffy. Stir in half the flour with the coffee and half the milk. Add remaining flour and milk and beat until mixture is smooth.

Pour into prepared tin and bake for approximately 25 minutes or until skewer comes out clean when tested. Leave in tin for about 15 minutes before turning out on to a rack to cool completely.

To make the filling, mix together the mascarpone, icing sugar, vanilla, orange zest and juice and the milk until you have a smooth and creamy mixture. Drain the cherries and reserve some of the liquid.

To assemble, crumble half the coffee cake into the bottom of a glass serving bowl and sprinkle with about 4-5 tablespoons of the reserved syrup. Top with half the cherries and half the mascarpone mixture.

Repeat this process, finishing off with a layer of the mascarpone mixture. Sprinkle the top with cocoa and decorate with the chocolate shavings. Refrigerate overnight before serving.

Serves 8-10

Pear and Chocolate Puddings

1 cup quinoa flour

½ tsp bicarbonate of soda (baking soda)

½ tsp baking powder

2/3 cup caster (superfine) sugar

3 tbsp cocoa powder

1 tsp instant coffee powder

150 g (5 oz) butter, very soft

2 eggs

2 tsp vanilla extract

2 tbsp milk

1 x 825 g (28¾ oz) can pears in juice, drained

Preheat oven to 180°C (350°F) and lightly grease four x 250 ml (9 fl oz) capacity ramekins.

Sift flour, bicarbonate of soda and baking powder together and place into a bowl with the sugar, cocoa, coffee, butter, eggs, vanilla and milk and beat with electric beaters until thick and smooth.

Place a spoonful of the mixture into the bottom of each ramekin.

Slice the pears and divide equally between the four ramekins then spoon the remainder of the chocolate mixture evenly over the pears.

Tap the ramekins on a counter top to release any air bubbles and bake for about 15–20 minutes depending on how fudgy and soft you like the centre to be.

Remove from oven and serve warm or cold with a dusting of icing sugar.

Serves 4

Quinoa Biscuits

Preheat oven to 180°C (350°F) and line two baking trays with non-stick baking paper.

Place quinoa flakes, flour, sugar and baking powder into a bowl then stir in the coconut.

Melt butter and golden syrup in a small saucepan, add the vanilla then stir in the bicarbonate of soda and water. Mixture may froth up when you add the soda so make sure saucepan is not too small.

Mix the butter mixture with the dry ingredients until thoroughly combined.

Place spoonfuls of cookie mixture onto prepared trays and bake for approximately 10 minutes or until golden. Cool completely on the trays.

These biscuits keep well in an airtight container.

1 cup quinoa flakes
1 cup quinoa flour
1 cup caster (superfine) sugar
1 tsp baking powder
¾ cup desiccated coconut
125g (4oz) butter
1½ tbsp golden syrup
1 tsp vanilla extract
1 tsp bicarbonate of soda (baking soda)
2 tbsp boiling water

Makes 20–24 biscuits

Note: These can be enjoyed with a cup of tea or coffee.

Apricot and Coconut Slice

Preheat oven to 180°C (350°F).

Sift flour and baking powder into a large bowl. Add the quinoa flakes, coconut, sugar and the chopped apricots. Stir in the melted butter and mix thoroughly to combine. Make sure all the ingredients are completely coated with the butter.

Press the apricot mixture firmly into an ungreased, non-stick 27 x 17 cm (10½ x 6½ in) slice tin.

Bake for 20–25 minutes or until a golden brown colour.

Remove from the oven, cool for 5 minutes and, while still warm, cut into 16 pieces, then cool completely in the tin before storing in an airtight container.

Makes 16 pieces

Note: This slice keeps well in an airtight container for two to three weeks, although it is usually eaten long before that.

½ cup quinoa flour
1 tsp gluten-free baking powder
1 cup quinoa flakes
1 cup shredded coconut
¾ cup raw (Demerara/turbinado) sugar
200 g (7 oz) dried apricots, chopped
150 g (5 oz) butter, melted

Baked Apples with Sultanas, Walnuts and Cinnamon

6 large Granny Smith apples

½ cup quinoa flakes

125 g (4 oz) sultanas

60 g (2 oz) walnuts, chopped

3 tbsp brown sugar

2 tsp ground cinnamon

1 tsp vanilla extract

1 tbsp butter

1 cup water

1 tsp icing (confectioners') sugar, extra
custard or ice-cream, for serving

Preheat oven to 180°C (350°F).

Core the apples then make a shallow cut through the skin around the circumference of each apple. This stops them from bursting during cooking. If apples are uneven, cut off a very thin slice from the bottom of each so that they sit straight in the dish.

Mix together the quinoa flakes, sultanas, walnuts, sugar, cinnamon and vanilla. Lightly rub in the butter.

Fill each apple with the mixture and place in a baking dish. Pour the water into the dish and bake for approximately 1 hour.

Spoon any pan juices over the apples, sprinkle with a little icing sugar and serve warm or cold with ice-cream or custard.

Serves 6

Note: I have always thought that there is something very magical and comforting about the smell of cooked apples and cinnamon as it wafts through the house.

Mixed Berry Crumble

500 g (17½ oz) frozen mixed berries,
  thawed
¼ cup brown sugar, tightly packed

TOPPING
½ cup quinoa flour
1 tsp gluten-free baking powder
½ cup quinoa flakes
½ cup brown sugar, tightly packed
1 tsp ground cinnamon
2 tsp vanilla extract
100 g (3½ oz) butter, at room
  temperature
3 tbsp flaked almonds
icing (confectioners') sugar, for serving
custard or ice-cream, for serving

Preheat oven to 180°C (350°F).

Mix the frozen berries with the sugar and place in an oven-proof dish.

Make the topping by sifting together the quinoa flour and baking powder and placing in a bowl with the quinoa flakes, sugar, cinnamon and vanilla. Lightly rub in the butter until the mixture resembles coarse breadcrumbs.

Cover the berries with the crumble mixture then scatter the almonds on top.

Bake for about 25–30 minutes until bubbly and golden. Cool and serve either warm or cold with a dusting of icing sugar and ice-cream.

Serves 4–6

Lime Tart

Preheat oven to 170°C (335°F) and brush a round 20 x 4 cm (8 x 1½ in) non-stick cake tin with butter and line the base of the tin with non-stick baking paper.

Sift the flour, baking powder and bicarbonate of soda into a bowl, add sugar and stir well to combine.

Using your fingertips, rub the butter into the flour until the mixture resembles fine breadcrumbs.

Lightly whisk the egg with the vanilla extract then stir into the flour mixture until you get a soft dough that holds together.

Using your fingers, press two-thirds of the dough into the base of the baking tin allowing the dough to come halfway up the sides of the tin. Pour the hot filling into the tin.

Take pieces of the remaining pastry and press between your fingertips to form small discs the size of a small coin and place over filling.

Bake for about 25 minutes until the top is golden. Cool completely in tin before transferring to a serving platter. Dust with icing sugar before serving.

To make the filling, combine all ingredients in a small saucepan and stir constantly over low heat until mixture starts to bubble and thicken.

1 cup quinoa flour
1 tsp gluten-free baking powder
1 tsp bicarbonate of soda (baking soda)
½ cup caster (superfine) sugar
60 g (2 oz) butter
1 extra large egg
1 tsp vanilla extract
icing (confectioner's) sugar, for dusting

FILLING
60 g (2 oz) butter
¼ cup lime juice
½ cup sugar
1 extra large egg

Serves 6

Note: This is another family favourite and I'm sure it will become one of yours too.

159

Coffee and Chocolate Butter Cake

3 tbsp instant coffee

3 tbsp boiling water

1½ cups quinoa flour

1½ tsp gluten-free baking powder

1½ tsp bicarbonate of soda (baking soda)

2 tbsp cocoa powder

125 g (4 oz) butter, softened

2 tsp vanilla extract

1 cup caster (superfine) sugar

2 extra large eggs

⅓ cup milk

chocolate shavings, to decorate

fresh strawberries (optional),
  to decorate

COFFEE ICING

2 tbsp instant coffee powder

2 tbsp boiling water

125 g (4 oz) butter

1 tsp vanilla extract

2 cups icing (confectioners') sugar,
  sifted

2 tsp milk

Preheat oven to 160°C (325°F) and grease two 20 cm (8 in) round non-stick cake tins.

Dissolve the coffee in the boiling water and set aside. Sift flour, baking powder, bicarbonate of soda and cocoa.

Cream butter, vanilla and sugar together until creamy. Add the eggs, one at a time, and beat until light and fluffy.

Stir in half the flour with the coffee and half the milk.

Add remaining flour and milk and beat until mixture is smooth. Divide cake mixture between the two prepared tins, tap tins on kitchen counter to release any air bubbles, then bake for approximately 25 minutes or until skewer comes out clean when tested.

Leave cakes in tin for about 15 minutes before turning out on to a wire rack to cool completely.

When cakes have cooled, sandwich them together with half the coffee icing. Decorate top layer with remaining icing and decorate with chocolate shavings and strawberries if using.

To make the icing, dissolve the coffee in the water and allow to cool. Beat the butter and vanilla in a bowl until light and creamy. Add the icing sugar, coffee and milk and beat for 2-3 minutes until smooth and fluffy.

Serves 8

Apple Pie

Place the flour, salt, baking powder, bicarb, cinnamon and sugar in a food processor. Pulse for a few seconds then add the butter and vanilla and pulse until the mixture resembles fine breadcrumbs. With the motor running, add the water, a little at a time, until the dough comes together. Turn onto a floured surface and shape into a flat disc. Wrap in plastic wrap and refrigerate for at least 1 hour.

Mix all the filling ingredients together.

Preheat the oven to 160°C (325°F) and grease a 20 cm (8 in) round pie tin with butter.

Divide the pastry into two pieces and place on a sheet of non-stick baking paper (makes the pastry much easier to transfer to the tin). Roll one piece of pastry to cover the base and sides of the pie tin and the other (a smaller piece) to use as a lid. Roll out and line the pie tin with pastry and fill with the apple mixture. Cover the pie with the pastry lid then lightly press and crimp the edges together to seal then cut three small vents on the top. Brush with beaten egg and bake for about 50–55 minutes until golden.

Cool before slicing and serve with ice-cream or custard. The pie is best served on the day of baking.

2½ cups quinoa flour
¼ tsp salt
1¼ tsp baking powder
½ tsp bicarbonate of soda (baking soda)
1 tsp ground cinnamon
½ cup caster (superfine) sugar
150 g (5 oz) very cold, unsalted butter, cut into pieces
2 tsp vanilla extract
½ cup icy cold water
1 egg, beaten

FILLING
1 x 800 g (28 oz) can pie apples
1 tsp cinnamon
⅓ cup sultanas
½ cup brown sugar

Serves 6–8

Note: Tinned pie apples work best in this recipe. You can use fresh apples if you prefer (about 1 kg/ 2 lb 4 oz) of apples peeled and thinly sliced). You will also need to adjust the amount of sugar.

THE KIDS' TABLE

Crunchy Chicken Bites

500 g (17½ oz) chicken breast fillets
1¼ cup quinoa flakes
1 tbsp ground sweet paprika
1½ tbsp sesame seeds
salt, to taste
1 tbsp extra virgin olive oil
1 egg, lightly beaten

Preheat oven to 190°C (375°F) and line a large baking tray with non-stick baking paper.

Trim the chicken fillets and cut into long, thick strips then cube into bite-sized pieces.

Mix together the flakes, paprika, sesame seeds, salt and oil.

Dip all the chicken pieces into the beaten egg then coat them well by pressing into the flake mixture. Place on the baking tray, in a single layer, and bake for about 20–25 minutes until golden and crisp.

Serves 4-6

Note: This crunchy coating also works well with fish, preferably a boneless fish.

166

Creamy Porridge

½ cup quinoa flakes
1½ cups milk
½ cup water
2 tbsp brown sugar
1 tsp vanilla extract
2-3 tbsp sultanas

Place quinoa flakes, milk, water, sugar and vanilla into a saucepan and stir well.

Add the sultanas and bring to the boil on medium heat. When boiling, reduce heat to low and simmer for about 5-7 minutes until thick and creamy.

Serves 2

Note: You could leave the sultanas out and add mashed banana or grated apple instead or even just a sprinkle of ground cinnamon.

Pizza

Preheat oven to 200°C (400°F).

Sift flour into a bowl with the baking powder and bicarb, stir in the oregano, parmesan and salt then make a well in the centre.

Pour the water and oil in the well and with the tips of your fingers slowly incorporate the flour with the oil and water until the mixture comes together and you have a workable dough. If the dough is too dry, add a little more water.

Place onto a floured surface and shape into a flat disc. Place the disc on a sheet of non-stick baking paper and roll out the pastry into a thin free-form round or square shape. If the pastry splits along the edges as you roll it out, just pinch the sides together. Then place the baking paper with the pizza base on it onto a baking tray. The pastry is much easier to handle and move around if on baking paper. Bake the pizza base for 15 minutes.

In the meantime, prepare the topping by mixing together tomato paste, garlic, herbs and olive oil.

Remove pizza base from the oven and spread evenly with the topping.

Top with the basil leaves, olives and lastly the mozzarella cheese. Bake for another 8–10 minutes.

This pizza is best eaten straight away.

Serves 2

1½ cups quinoa flour
1 tsp baking powder
½ tsp bicarbonate of soda (baking soda)
½ tsp ground oregano
2 tbsp parmesan, grated
1 tsp garlic salt
½ cup warm water plus 1 tbsp
2 tbsp extra virgin olive oil

TOPPING
3 tbsp tomato paste (concentrate)
1 clove garlic, finely grated
1 tsp dried Italian herbs
2 tsps extra virgin olive oil
5–6 large basil leaves, torn
10–12 pitted Kalamata olives, sliced or halved
¾ cup mozzarella cheese, shredded

169

'Mac' and Cheese

Preheat oven to 200°C (400°F).

Place the quinoa in a saucepan with the water, bring to the boil, reduce heat, cover and simmer for 10 minutes until all the water is absorbed. Cool.

Place the quinoa, ricotta and peas into a large bowl and season with salt and pepper.

To make the sauce, melt butter, stir in mustard then stir in flour and cook for a few seconds until butter and flour are well incorporated and a roux is formed.

Slowly pour in the milk and whisk continuously until the sauce thickens and starts to bubble. Stir in the cheeses, taste and adjust the seasoning if necessary and cook until cheese melts.

Pour the white cheese sauce over the quinoa mixture and gently mix to thoroughly combine. Pour into an oven-proof dish, sprinkle with some extra grated cheese and ground paprika and bake for about 30–40 minutes until golden.

Serves 6–8

1½ cups quinoa, rinsed and drained
3 cups water
250 g (9 oz) ricotta, crumbled
1½ cups frozen peas, thawed
salt and freshly ground black pepper
handful of tasty or mild cheddar cheese, grated, extra
ground sweet paprika, for garnish

CHEESE SAUCE
125 g (4 oz) butter
1 tbsp mild English mustard
½ cup quinoa flour
5 cups milk
1 cup tasty or mild cheddar cheese, grated
½ cup parmesan, grated
salt and freshly ground black pepper (optional)

Spaghetti Bolognaise

1-2 tbsp olive oil
1 medium onion, finely chopped
500 g (17½ oz) minced (ground) beef
2 cloves garlic, finely chopped
1 tbsp tomato paste (concentrate)
½ tsp sugar
1 x 400 g (14 oz) can diced tomatoes, undrained
1½ tsp dried oregano
salt and pepper
2 cups hot water
parmesan, grated, for serving

FRESH QUINOA PASTA DOUGH
500 g (17½ oz) quinoa flour
¼ tsp salt
5 extra large eggs
1 tbsp olive oil

Heat oil in a large saucepan and sauté onion until soft and lightly browned. Add the beef and continue cooking until beef is browned, making sure to break up any lumps.

Stir in the garlic, cook for 30 seconds then stir in the tomato paste and sugar and cook for 1-2 minutes, stirring regularly.

Add the tomatoes, oregano, salt and pepper and cook until the sauce starts to bubble. Pour in the water, stir well, bring to the boil then reduce the heat, cover and simmer for about 40-45 minutes until the sauce has reduced and thickened. Add more water if the sauce dries out too quickly during cooking.

Serve over quinoa spaghetti and add a good sprinkling of grated parmesan before serving.

To make the spaghetti, place all ingredients into a food processor and process until the dough comes together.

Knead lightly on a floured board, wrap the dough in plastic and let it rest in the fridge for about 30 minutes before you start rolling and cutting (as per your pasta machine instructions or by hand). Pasta dough will be dark in colour but will lighten as it cooks.

Cook the pasta in lots of boiling, salted water but watch cooking time as this pasta cooks fairly quickly.

Serves 4-6

quinoa for families

Mini Banana Muffins

Preheat oven to 170°C (335°F) and line two 24-cup mini muffin tin with paper cases.

Mash the bananas with the lemon juice and set aside.

Sift together the flour, sugar, bicarbonate of soda, baking powder and salt into a large bowl. Pour milk into a jug then lightly beat in the eggs, vanilla and oil.

Make a well in the centre of the dry ingredients and slowly pour in the liquid ingredients mixing as you go until all the ingredients are combined.

Gently fold in the bananas; do not over mix.

Spoon the mixture into the prepared muffin tin filling each case fairly close to the top and cover with a thin slice of banana, if using.

Bake for about 20 minutes until they have risen, are golden and firm to the touch and skewer comes out clean when tested.

Makes 48 mini muffins

Note: These muffins are great for school lunches. This recipe makes a lot of mini muffins but they freeze really well. Just pop a frozen one in their school lunches. They are lovely eaten warm or cold and will remain fresh and moist for 3–4 days—kids love them.

2 overripe bananas
2 tsp lemon juice
2 cups quinoa flour
1 cup caster (superfine) sugar
1 level tsp bicarbonate of soda (baking soda)
½ level tsp gluten-free baking powder
⅓ tsp salt
¾ cup milk
2 large eggs
2 tsp vanilla paste or extract
¼ cup vegetable or extra light olive oil
1 banana, for garnish (optional)

Ham, Corn and Pea Bakes

Place quinoa in a small saucepan with the water, bring to the boil, then reduce the heat, cover and simmer for 10 minutes until all the water is absorbed. Remove from the heat and cool.

Preheat oven to 190°C (375°F) and grease 10–12 small non-stick different-shaped decorative ovenproof moulds or a 12-hole non-stick muffin pan.

Place quinoa into a bowl with the corn, peas, ham, capsicum and cheese.

Whisk the eggs and milk together, season with salt and pepper then pour into the quinoa mixture and mix until well combined.

Spoon the mixture into the prepared baking moulds/muffin pan, filling each one to the top.

Bake for approximately 25–30 minutes until set and golden. Cool for about 10 minutes before removing from the tins.

½ cup quinoa, rinsed and drained
1 cup water
1 cup frozen corn, thawed
1 cup frozen peas, thawed
90 g (3 oz) ham or bacon, chopped
½ red capsicum (pepper), finely diced
1 cup tasty or cheddar cheese, grated
3 extra large eggs
½ cup milk
salt and pepper

Makes 10–12 individual bakes

Note: I like to add a tablespoon of Dijon or English mustard into the mixture before baking especially if I am making these for the adults. The adult 'kids' also like pancetta or salami as an alternative to ham or bacon. For this recipe, I usually use ovenproof silicon trays that are made up of different shapes that kids love, such as dinosaurs, flowers and trains.

the kids' table

Sweet Pizza

1 cup quinoa flour
¾ tsp baking powder
½ tsp ground cinnamon
1 tbsp caster (superfine) sugar
½ tsp vanilla extract
4–5 tbsp water
2 tbsp extra light olive oil
3 tbsp choc-hazelnut spread
fresh strawberries ,sliced
bananas, sliced
1–2 tbsp hazelnut spread, extra

Preheat oven to 200°C (400°F).

Sift flour into a bowl with the baking powder, stir in the cinnamon and sugar then make a well in the centre.

Pour in the water and oil in the well and with the tips of your fingers slowly incorporate the flour with the oil and water until you have a dough that is not sticky. If need be, add a little more flour.

Once the dough is workable, roll it out into a thin free-form round or square shape on to a piece of non-stick baking paper. If the pastry splits along the edges as you roll it out, just pinch the sides together. Move the baking paper and pizza base onto a baking tray. The pastry is much easier to handle and move around if on baking paper.

Bake for 8–10 minutes then remove from the oven and spread with the hazelnut spread. Top with strawberries and slices of banana. Heat the extra hazelnut spread in the microwave until runny and drizzle over the pizza. Cut into eight wedges.

Serves 4–8

Pikelets (Small Pancakes)

Sift the flour with the baking powder, bicarbonate of soda and salt into a bowl then stir in the sugar.

Mix together the milk, lemon juice, vanilla, egg and melted butter.

Pour the wet ingredients into the dry ingredients and whisk into a smooth batter.

Heat a non-stick frying pan (you may need to lightly grease the pan) on medium heat then drop spoonfuls of the batter into the pan.

When bubbles start to appear and the pikelet has set on the bottom, flip over and cook on the other side for about 20 seconds—just long enough for the top to seal.

Remove from the pan and serve while still warm with your favourite topping, such as jam, honey or maple syrup.

1 cup quinoa flour
3/4 tsp gluten-free baking powder
3/4 tsp bicarbonate of soda (baking soda)
1/4 tsp salt
3 tbsp caster (superfine) sugar
2/3 cup milk
1 tsp lemon juice
2 tsp vanilla extract
1 extra large egg
1 tbsp butter, melted

Makes 15-18 pikelets

Note: For a savoury pikelet, leave out the sugar and vanilla and add some grated cheese or chopped ham instead.

the kids' table

Chocolate Chip Cookies on a Stick

1½ cups quinoa flour
1 tsp gluten-free baking powder
½ tsp bicarbonate of soda
¼ tsp salt
180 g (6 oz) chocolate chips
125 g (4 oz) butter, softened
¼ cup brown sugar
⅓ cup caster (superfine) sugar
2 tsp vanilla extract
2 extra large eggs
wooden ice-cream/lollipop sticks

Preheat the oven to 180°C (350°F) and line two baking trays with non-stick baking paper.

Sift together the flour, baking powder, bicarbonate of soda and salt, stir in the chocolate chips and set aside.

Cream the butter, brown sugar and caster sugar together until light and creamy.

Beat in the vanilla and eggs then fold into the flour mixture until well combined. Mixture will be a little soft and sticky.

Place spoonfuls of cookie dough the size of a large walnut onto a baking tray then insert a wooden stick into the centre of the cookie.

Bake for about 11–12 minutes. Biscuits should not be overcooked and still be a little soft when taken out of the oven.

Cool biscuits completely in the tray before attempting to remove them.

Makes about 15 cookies

Note: If making for gluten/wheat intolerant people, chocolate chips should be checked that they are wheat/gluten free.

Chocolate Brownies

Preheat oven to 180°C (350°F) and lightly grease a 24 cm (9½ in) square non-stick baking tin.

Sift cocoa into a bowl and stir in the coffee and sugar.

Whisk together the butter, eggs and vanilla then slowly mix in the cocoa and sugar mixture.

Sift the flour with the baking powder and salt, add to the chocolate mixture and mix until thoroughly combined.

Fold in the walnuts and chocolate chips and pour into the prepared tin. Give the tin a good tap on your kitchen counter to release any air bubbles before placing in the oven and baking for about 25 minutes.

Cool in the tin before turning out. Dust with icing sugar before cutting.

Makes 12 brownies

Note: If making for gluten/wheat intolerant people, chocolate chips should be checked that they are wheat/gluten free.

¾ cup cocoa powder
1 tsp instant coffee
1½ cups sugar
180 g (6 oz) butter, melted
4 extra large eggs
2 tsp vanilla extract
¾ cups quinoa flour
2 tsp gluten-free baking powder
pinch of salt
1 cup walnuts, chopped
1 cup chocolate chips
icing (confectioners') sugar, for dusting

Strawberry Banana Jelly

¼ cup quinoa, rinsed and drained
¾ cup water
1 tsp vanilla extract
2 x 85g (3 oz) packet strawberry jelly
2 cups boiling water
2 medium bananas

Place quinoa in a small saucepan with the water and vanilla, bring to the boil, then reduce the heat, cover and simmer for 10 minutes until all the water is absorbed. Remove from heat and cool completely.

Prepare the jelly by dissolving with the boiling water and cool until tepid.

Lightly spray a 20 cm (8 in) loaf tin with cooking spray and line with plastic food wrap.

Mix the quinoa into the jelly and stir well, breaking up any lumps that may form. Pour into the prepared tin and stand for about 5 minutes until the quinoa settles to the bottom of the tin.

Place the banana slices into the jelly, making sure they are coated in jelly to prevent them from browning. It doesn't matter if they float to the top.

Place in refrigerator to completely set. Slowly lift the jelly out of the tin with the plastic and then very gently slide the jelly off the plastic and onto a serving dish or slowly invert the tin onto a serving platter so the quinoa ends up on top, then remove the plastic. Cut into slices and serve. Keep jelly refrigerated until just before serving.

Serves 6

Note: You might think this is an odd dish, but it is just something fun I thought of when trying to come up with different ways to use quinoa. You could change the jelly flavour and use other fruit like grapes, cherries, strawberries, peaches or nectarines.

Acknowledgements

A huge thank you to my publisher, Linda Williams—without her belief in me and this wonderful grain, this book and my first quinoa book, *Cooking with Quinoa*, would never have happened.

Thank you also to Fiona Schultz, Lliane Clarke and all the team at New Holland—Sacha Gratton, Christine Roberts, Diane Ward and especially my beautiful editor Jodi De Vantier—for all their help and support throughout the whole process of publishing my books.

Thank you to my wonderful photographer Graeme Gillies and stylist Mandy Biffin for giving life to my cooking.

Lastly, but certainly not least, to all my family for their constant love and support and never complaining about eating whatever I cook. I love you.

To my beautiful, sweet Buffy. I miss you so much. The long hours spent writing on the computer will never be the same again. xxx

INDEX

quinoa for families

189

191

index

First published in 2012 by

New Holland Publishers Pty Ltd

London • Sydney • Cape Town • Auckland

Garfield House 86–88 Edgware Road London W2 2EA United Kingdom

1/66 Gibbes Street Chatswood NSW 2067 Australia

218 Lake Road Northcote Auckland New Zealand

Wembley Square First Floor Solan Road Gardens Cape Town 8001 South Africa

www.newhollandpublishers.com

www.newholland.com.au

A catalogue record of this book is available at the British Library.

A record of this book is held at the National Library of Australia

ISBN 9781742572352

Publisher: Linda Williams

Publishing director: Lliane Clarke

Project editor: Jodi De Vantier

Designer: Tracy Loughlin

Photographs: Graeme Gillies

Food stylist: Amanda Biffin

Cover and ends texture: www.myfreetextures.com

Production director: Olga Dementiev

Printer: Toppan Leefung Printing Ltd

10 9 8 7 6 5 4

Keep up with New Holland Publishers on Facebook and Twitter.

www.facebook.com/NewHollandPublishers